"In *Renegade*, Vince Antonucci will make you laugh out loud, tug at your heart with inspiring real-life stories, and challenge you to live a daring adventure with God."

Mark Batterson, pastor of National Community Church in Washington, DC, and author of *The Circle Maker*

"If you are tired of a mediocre faith, Vince Antonucci's book *Renegade* will inspire you to an all-in, fully surrendered, self-sacrificing faith journey with Christ."

Craig Groeschel, pastor of LifeChurch.tv and author of *Soul Detox*

"Vince Antonucci's writing always challenges me while making me laugh. In *Renegade*, he pushes all of us to live with radical faith in a radical God. Vince does more than write this story, he lives it and gives us a compelling picture for what the life of faith looks like."

Jud Wilhite, pastor of Central Christian Church in Las Vegas and author of *Torn*

"The message of *Renegade* will teach you, entertain you, inspire you, challenge you, and convict you. . . . My prayer is that this book starts a movement of renegades who turn the world upside down."

Kyle Idleman, teaching pastor at Southeast Christian Church in Louisville, KY, and author of *Not a Fan*

"If you are tired of a play-it-safe, go-through-the-motions faith, then *Renegade* is exactly what you need. Authored by a guy who is a serial risk-taker, this book will have you laughing while at the same time discovering that faith was always meant to be a daring adventure! *Renegade* is a book for all of us who want a faith that is more than knowing what Jesus would do, but rather doing what he would do!"

Dave Ferguson, pastor of Community Christian Church and coauthor of *Exponential*

RENEGADE

YOUR FAITH ISN'T MEANT
TO BE SAFE

VINCE
ANTONUCCI

BakerBooks

a division of Baker Publishing Group
Grand Rapids, Michigan

Published by Baker Books
a division of Baker Publishing Group
P.O. Box 6287, Grand Rapids, MI 49516-6287
www.bakerbooks.com

Printed in the United States of America

Library of Congress Cataloging-in-Publication Data
Antonucci, Vince.
    Renegade : your faith isn't meant to be safe / Vince Antonucci.
        p.   cm.
    Includes bibliographical references. (pages   )
    ISBN 978-0-8010-1501-4 (pbk.)
    1. Christian life. I. Title.
BV4501.3.A585 2013
248.4—dc23   2012041204

13   14   15   16   17   18   19   8   7   6   5   4   3   2

Boredom is the root of all evil.

Søren Kierkegaard

Contents

Contents

Foreword

How do you really know you are following Jesus?

Most of us are quick to point to evidence like our family heritage, our church attendance, or the rules we've kept and religious rituals we've followed. You might talk about a decision you made at church camp when, after singing the invitation song for thirty minutes, you were the only who hadn't cracked, and it was then you finally stepped across the line. You might try to demonstrate your biblical knowledge by quoting John 3:16 or Psalm 23. But the most basic definition of following someone is that you go where they go.

So maybe that's a better way to ask the question. Instead of asking, "Are you following Jesus?" the question should be, "Are you going where Jesus went? Are you doing what Jesus did? Are you loving who Jesus loved?"

Instead of just saying yes and showing me your tattoo written in Hebrew or pointing out that your Facebook status says Christ-follower, I want to see if you can answer the question with a story.

Seriously. Can you tell me a story?

Not a story from the Bible that you learned when you were a kid. Not a story about someone else that was forwarded to you. Can you answer the question with a story that you're a part of? Tell me a story of *where* you have followed Jesus. Tell me

9

a story with the name of a person who you have been Jesus to. Tell me a story about a risk you took following Jesus.

The first time I met Vince Antonucci was in 1998 at a church-planting conference. Somehow we ended up as roommates. Vince had planted a church in Virginia Beach that had exploded. I, on the other hand, was twenty-two years old and was considering planting a church only because I needed a job and no one was interested in hiring a young preacher with no experience. It had become clear that the only way I would be able to preach at a church was to plant one.

I arrived at the hotel and headed up to my room. When I opened the door, Vince was on his bed surrounded by dozens and dozens of 8 x 10 colored cards. After we introduced ourselves, I asked him what he was doing. He explained to me that he was praying through the cards, and that each card contained the name and contact information of someone whose life was changed at the church that he started. He then proceeded to go through a number of the cards, reading the person's name and then passionately telling me their story. I remember thinking, *These stories are incredible! I either need to think of one quick or make one up!*

I was challenged more by him in those few minutes than I was during the rest of the conference. His stories and his passion made me want to plant a church and follow Jesus in such a way that I could tell stories like that. And as I read *Renegade*, I found myself being convicted and challenged by his passion and his stories all over again.

The message of *Renegade* will teach you, entertain you, inspire you, challenge you, and convict you; and that's great, but if that's all it does then you will have missed the point of this book. I have prayed for you as you read this book, and my prayer is that this book would be much more than a message. My prayer is that it starts a movement of renegades who turn the world upside down.

Oh yeah. One more thing before you start this journey. Just for the record: I am not the friend you will read about in chapter 3.

Kyle Idleman

PART 1

INTIMACY WITH GOD, INFLUENCE IN THE WORLD

Welcome.

In this section you'll be introduced to a Las Vegas fire-breathing atheistic clown and a Beverly Hills radical nun. You will experience, disturbing blow by disturbing blow, the worst first date in the history of dating.

And, most importantly, you'll discover what it means to be a renegade for God, why you want to be one, and how you can.

1

Beware the Fire-Breathing Atheist

He swaggered in wearing both a scowl and bad intentions. By profession, Warren was an evil fire-breathing clown in a horror show in Las Vegas. He also moonlighted as a freak-show wrestler.

By philosophy, Warren was an atheist—a hard-core atheist. A "There is no God, and if there was one I would hate him, and I despise anyone who believes there is a God or who tries to lead others to believe there is one" kind of atheist.

Warren heard about this new church starting in his city. He thought his city, a city that prides itself on sin, was no place for someone to start a new church. He decided to do something about it.

He realized a new church wouldn't have many people and that the people who did show up would not be very committed, which helped him form his plan: he would go to one of the church's first services, sit in the middle of the room, and wait. When the pastor walked onstage to give the sermon, Warren would stand up and let loose a barrage of profanity, throw some chairs, and hopefully hit the pastor and maybe a few others as well. He figured that all the people who were still making up their minds about the church would decide, "If I have to subject myself to this, forget it!" and never come back. The church wouldn't be able to survive without people, and Warren could brag for the rest of his life that he had killed a church.

It was a great plan. There was just one problem: I was the pastor.

Called to Be a Renegade

I grew up in a completely non-Christian home. My mother was Jewish and my father was a professional poker player. I knew nothing about God or Jesus or the Bible or Christianity. I had never been to church, and as far as I knew, I had never met a Christian.

At the age of twenty I started reading the Bible because I thought I could prove it wasn't true. Whoops. I soon encountered volumes of evidence proving otherwise. But even more than the evidence, what turned my head was Jesus. He was the most amazing person I had ever encountered. So amazing, in fact, that he couldn't be just a person. He lived a radically different life and invited people into an upside-down kingdom.

People who said yes in the Bible had their lives *inverted*. They realized that everything they had been taught, everything they had lived, was wrong. They went from selfish to selfless, from having grudge-inspired thoughts of revenge to loving their enemies through acts of kindness, from playing it safe to playing it dangerous. I mean, the theme of Jesus's promotional campaign was, "To follow me you must carry a cross." Everyone knew what that meant. A man only carried a cross to his death.*

Outsiders looked at how Christians lived and called them idiots, and the Christians didn't exactly disagree, referring to themselves as fools for Christ and the refuse of the world.†

---

*Can you imagine if churches today sent out postcards that, instead of promising "Relevant Teaching! Contemporary Worship! Fun Children's Programming!" simply said, "Come and Die"?

†Again, I want to see the church postcard: "Come join us, we're crap!"

I saw all of this and realized I couldn't say no. I couldn't say no to this homeless king and his wrong-side-up kingdom. And honestly, I was afraid. What might that yes mean? What would my life look like? What might I have to do for God? It was the most dangerous decision I had ever made, but I took a deep breath and said yes.

That was when I started meeting Christians. I wondered if we were reading the same Bible. They were all nice people, but I couldn't tell if their lives had been inverted and wasn't sure "fools for Christ" was the best description for them. It didn't seem like outsiders would call them idiots. No, probably they would call them . . . respectable. Maybe even dignified.

The problem was that I had read the Bible. I knew Christians weren't people who behaved and dressed right and had good manners. Jesus didn't get crucified for being respectable. He was crucified because he was viewed as a crazy man leading an uncivilized revolution, and that is a dangerous thing. You have to get rid of a guy like that. I knew that God does not call his followers to be dignified. He calls us to faith, and faith is *always* dangerous. Faith always feels like risk. God doesn't call us to be the same as everyone else. He calls us to be different. He calls us to the lunatic fringe. He calls us to be renegades.

A renegade is a person who rejects conventional behavior, who refuses to do what others are doing, and who realizes there's a different beat they can dance to—and it's *better*. Once they start walking their unique path others may follow, but at first it can be lonely. But that's okay, because a renegade realizes "normal" isn't working for anyone else, nor is it working for them. So they abandon normal to find *right*. It isn't easy, but it's the only way to truly live for God.

It isn't easy because it requires something radical from us. God isn't looking for the halfhearted or the lukewarm. Anywhere we look in the Bible, we see that we are meant to be all-in when it comes to following Jesus. We *know* that, and we want to make that commitment. So we say yes, but it's a yes with lots of buts.

Jesus said we're to love God with all our hearts and everything we are, *but* it's easier to love God in a more subdued way.

We love him, but we're not going to go overboard and get weird about it. We're not going to risk being called idiots.

Jesus said that to love God is to obey his commands, *but* it's easier to obey his commands when it's convenient to do so and to ignore his commands when it's not.

Jesus said to be his witnesses, sharing our faith with people who don't know him, *but* that's awkward. It's easier to just pray that our friends and co-workers somehow come to Christ without us having to say anything.

Jesus said to store our treasures in heaven, investing our money in his kingdom, *but* we want lots of stuff for ourselves. It's easier to just give God a little and spend most of our money on ourselves.

Jesus said to love, pray for, and forgive our enemies, *but* our particular enemy really screwed us over, and we hate him and hope he dies. Okay, he doesn't have to die, but it'd be nice if he at least has to suffer. A lot.

Here's the issue: we get to choose whether we want to follow Jesus, but we don't get to choose what it looks like to follow Jesus.

We want to follow Jesus *and* we want to live nice, safe, comfortable lives that are "normal." That's a problem—because it doesn't work. You can't have both. Following Jesus means embracing a selfless, crazy, dangerous, God-obsessed life, and that's something most people refuse to do.

To follow Jesus, we need to become renegades. We need to refuse to do what others are doing. We need to reject conventional behavior. We need to abandon normal. It's not going to be easy, but it's the only way.

Think of a person in the Bible who believed in and followed God while living a safe, normal life. You can't. As your mind starts traveling from Genesis to Revelation, you'll think of:

> *Abraham*, who was asked by God to move his family, but wasn't told where he was going

Noah, who was asked to build a boat when it wasn't raining

Moses, who, though he was a fugitive from Egypt, marched into Egypt and demanded that Pharaoh let his people go because God told him to

Joshua, whom God asked to march around the city walls and blow a trumpet, expecting the walls to fall down

Rahab, the prostitute who risked her life to do the right thing

Isaiah, the prophet who, at God's command, walked around completely naked for three years

Hosea, a righteous man whom God told to marry a prostitute

And the beat goes on. Everyone who said yes to God had to embrace a bit of crazy. They had to leave "safe" behind because following God was dangerous. They became renegades.

Me, a Renegade?

It couldn't have been easy for them, and it won't be for us either. It certainly hasn't been for me. I don't think I'm a renegade by nature, but I've asked God to transform my nature. It's intimidating because I'm very ordinary, but I have an extraordinary God. I force myself to think about that a lot: I am connected to a supernatural God. I have supernatural power available to me, supernatural compassion that drives me, and a supernatural cause to advance. I may be totally normal, but when I said yes to Jesus, everything was inverted. My life began to look like that of a renegade.

I became a Christian just prior to my junior year of college. I planned on going to law school, so my senior year I took my LSATs and began applying. I quickly received several acceptance letters, but I will never forget the day I got *the* letter. A Top 20 law school was offering me a full academic scholarship. They would pay for everything: tuition, room, food, books, *everything*. I could graduate from law school without paying a dime and without accruing loans. I said yes and soon discovered the average first-year salary coming out of this law school was $80,000. Cha-ching! And this was back in 1992.

So after completing my undergrad degree, I went to that law school, loved it, and got straight As. But the summer after my first year, I just knew I wasn't supposed to go back. Instead I was supposed to go to seminary to become a pastor. At seminary I would have to pay about $15,000 a year and wouldn't receive a scholarship. I didn't have any money, so it meant about $30,000 in loans. I did some research, and the average first-year salary for a pastor out of seminary was around $20,000. Cha-*what*? But it was clear this was what God wanted me to do.

After seminary I did an internship at a huge church of over ten thousand people. As the internship drew to a close, the church let me know I could become a full-time staff member, and I learned my salary would be about $40,000. Twice as much as I was counting on! And this church was located in an inexpensive city. They also offered all kinds of benefits. Champagne wishes and caviar dreams!

But I had also been talking to another church. It was only two years old. They had a hundred people on a good day, but wanted to grow and felt they needed a second pastor. The church was in a *very* expensive city. They suggested a salary of $30,000, but then explained that they couldn't actually afford to pay me anything; I would have to raise my own funding. I couldn't imagine how my wife and I could exist there on less than $30,000. Kool-Aid wishes and scrambled egg dreams! So my options were an established, amazing church giving me $40,000 a year and full benefits, or a church giving me $0.00 and hoping I could raise my own salary of $30,000 with no benefits. The decision was obvious, until God spoke. He told me to take what I considered to be the dumb option. But the dumb option made sense, because I was to be a renegade.

After two years our church had grown from one hundred to over four hundred people, and I was informed that *finally* they would be able to pay me. So I left—not because I didn't want to get paid. I did! But God was speaking again, and he led my wife and me to Virginia Beach to start a new church. It was a scary proposition. We knew that eight out of ten new churches die within the first three years. And we knew *nothing* about church planting. I hadn't taken a class on it, or even read a book about it. It was crazy, but we felt it was something we should do for God, so we did it.

The church in Virginia Beach took off and grew to almost a thousand people. We loved it there. We loved the city, the beach, our house, our friends, our church. We decided to stay forever. We got enticing offers from other churches, including bigger churches offering higher salaries, but we said no. We were staying in Virginia Beach forever. But then, eleven years after moving us to Virginia, God spoke yet again. He didn't tell us to take one of those bigger churches with the higher salaries. No, he told us to take the high-risk path of starting *another new church*. This time we were to do it in one of the least likely places for a church to succeed in the United States—just off the Strip in the heart of Las Vegas.

When I began to understand where God was directing us, I called two of my pastor friends in Vegas. I told them I was moving out to join them in ministering to Sin City. They celebrated with me. Then I mentioned we wanted to start the church not out in the suburbs, where all the other churches were, but right around the Strip. They begged me not to. The first friend told me there was no chance of it working. He said, "You don't understand the Strip area. This cannot work. Start a church in the suburbs and you'll do great, but don't do this." The second friend told me the church would never have more than fifty people, and that my decision was "career suicide." I told a third pastor of my plans, and he responded, "If you do this, you'll either fail or you'll succeed and people will want you dead." I laughed. He said, "No, I'm not kidding. I know you, and I know what you'll do, who you'll reach. If you're successful in your mission, there will be people in Las Vegas who will want you dead."

So I had no chance of succeeding, and if somehow I did, I'd be on the hit list of Sin City's pimps and drug dealers? Pretty sobering conversations, and they would have deterred me—if God hadn't called us to be renegades.

We packed up our stuff, our kids, and our dog, moved across the country, and started a church just off the Strip.

And that brings us back to Warren.

Warren Shows Up

Warren is a big guy: about six two, 280 pounds. He looks intimidating with his shaved head and his body covered in tattoos, and he couldn't wait to see the scared looks he would get when he walked through the church door.

But he didn't get them. People smiled, welcomed him, said they were glad he was there. *They're trained well*, he thought.

He made his way to the auditorium, picked the seat from which he would unleash his attack, and sat down. He looked up at the big screen and realized the slides that were flashing on it were . . . funny. One appeared on the screen: "If you have a cell phone, please turn it off. But if you have a pacemaker, leave that sucker on!"

Whatever, Warren thought, and waited. Then the church band came out and he thought, *Okay, here we go*. But the band started playing a song he knew and liked. Totally confusing. Then a guy walked onstage, welcomed everyone, and explained that the day's theme was that we are spiritually dead, but Jesus came to bring God's love and to bring us life from death. Then he did a top ten list: the top ten signs you're dead. "You keep hearing organ music and people saying, 'He looks so natural.'" "Jim Morrison calls about lunch." "You haven't breathed in over twenty-four hours." Warren laughed.

But when the guy announced he was going to pray, and then the band would do some worship songs, Warren thought, *Okay, so this has not been what I expected, but now it's coming*. But the prayer made sense, and the band actually kind of rocked, and finally the service was over and the pastor guy said, "We'll see you next week," and Warren realized, *I forgot to do my thing! My whole plan! I got so engaged in the service, I forgot I came here to ruin it!*

Warren came back for the service the following week, and he came back for the service the week after that. Pretty soon he started coming to *all three* of our services, which were identical. By that time we had met, so I approached him and asked, "Dude, I don't really know you, but you've got to be smart enough to realize that all three services are the same. Why do you come to all three of them?" And this fire-breathing, freak-show, hard-core atheist said, "I know. I just . . . I just can't get enough of Jesus."

A couple months later Warren stood in the parking lot behind our building. I handed him a microphone, because we always ask people who are about to be baptized to share their story beforehand. Warren pointed at the water in the kiddie pool in which he was about to be baptized (we do it up classy in Vegas), and he yelled: "I have a confession to make! I didn't come here for this. I came here because I hated you! I hated every single one of you, and I knew I was stronger than you!" His voice lowered. "But something happened to me here. I've learned that God loves me. And I don't understand that. But I just want more of it. And . . ." Warren couldn't continue, because what had started as a few sniffles and tears were now erupting in full-body sobs. He couldn't control himself. We took the mic away and lowered him into the water—and into the upside-down life Jesus called us to.

About a year later Warren still comes to every service, only now he shows up two hours early to clean the building before everyone else arrives. He is also in a discipleship group. Warren is broke, but he finds ways to give money to people in need. Warren's birthday was a month ago. He told all his friends he didn't want presents; instead he wanted them to come to our church's Monday night service. After the service we would have a birthday party, but they had to come to church first. Almost all of Warren's friends are atheists and Satanists who work in horror and freak shows. Thirty-four of them showed up. It was the strangest, scariest-looking church crowd in the history of church crowds. And one of the freaks kept coming back—and decided just this week he wants to go out back to the parking lot and immerse his life into the life of Jesus. It's all because of Warren.

Warren is a renegade.

You can be a renegade too.

2

Don't Live a Cheap Imitation

I meant to buy Apple Jacks. I was supposed to buy Apple Jacks. I thought I *did* buy Apple Jacks. When I grabbed the box. When I paid for it. When I took it out of the bag and put it on the counter. When I opened it and poured its contents into bowls. When I put the spoon to my mouth. But that's when I realized: it *wasn't* Apple Jacks. I looked again at the box: it said Apple *Macks*. I had been bamboozled!

You can hardly blame me. The boxes were right next to each other. They were the same height, same color, used the same font. But as I tasted what I had purchased, I knew I didn't have the real thing. Apple Macks was a close imitation, but it just wasn't quite *it*.

Maybe you've been duped by the breakfast food flimflam. It's an elaborate hoax pulled off by local grocery store chains hoping to scam you into buying their box of imitation cereal that's not quite the real thing.

Perhaps you bought a box of Apple Macks. Or thought you had Cocoa Puffs, only to discover they were Cocoa Poofs. Who hasn't been disappointed by a bowlful of not-so-great Skipper

Crunch? It's an easy mistake to make. They almost look the same; even the taste is close. But it's just not quite *it*.

Imitation Life

Do you think it's possible we've been duped into buying a cheap imitation of following God, and that has led us to live a cheap imitation life?

Your first response may be to roll your eyes. You know what you have, and it may not be perfect, but you *are* following God and it is "real life." But I also thought I knew I had Apple Jacks, and maybe the life we have is so close to the real thing that we assume it *is* the real thing. It doesn't taste quite as good as it's supposed to, but nothing ever lives up to expectations, right?

So let me ask you some questions.

How did you spend yesterday? Seriously, think about it. What time did you wake up? Where did you go when you left your place? What were the main events of the day? (You might even write them down.) When you returned home, what did you spend your time doing?

Looking back at that day, what about it would you say was truly God-centered? Joy-filled? Purpose-driven? Would you describe anything you did as adventurous or risky or dangerous? Is there anything happening in your life that truly requires faith? What are you doing that is only explainable by the fact that you believe in God and follow Jesus?

What if you looked honestly back at the last *month*, or looked forward to the next one? How much of it could be described as God-centered, joy-filled, purpose-driven, or adventurous?

For most of us the answer is, well, not much. We go through our day; we go through the motions; we eat our meals, watch our television, get in our beds, and the next day we do it all over again.

Is this all there is?

Seriously. Is what we're experiencing the life God intends for us? Think about this: we wouldn't waste our time daydreaming about the kind of life we're living, but we're willing to waste our *actual life* living it. Isn't there something wrong with that?

We want more, and God wants more for us.

Why do we allow ourselves to continue settling for a cheap imitation of the real thing?

Maybe it's because everyone else does. It just feels normal. Most of the people we know don't have the kind of relationship with God they really want either; they don't take many risks, and they are pretty bored with their lives. Living this way seems kind of expected and safe.

To find true fulfillment, to experience "all there is," we have to do something different. We have to stop playing it safe. We can't live the same way as everyone else anymore.

Renegade Life

If you look up the word *renegade*, you'll see it's not just someone who rejects conventional behavior. The word is often used for people who reject their religion. What if to truly find God and an adventurous life we need to abandon our religion? I'm not suggesting we walk away from God or the church or other believers. I'm saying that we leave behind the religious approach to God most of us take, which leads us to a cheap imitation of following him. We may not have to abandon our faith but rather abandon our way of *doing* faith—the way of faith we learned from our family, our friends, and what we've known before. We may have to go a bit rogue to find a religion-free relationship with God that leads to true intimacy with him and true influence in this world.

I realize this won't be easy.

It hasn't been for me. When I first said yes to the invitation of Jesus, I knew it meant being a renegade, but I live in a world that continually pulls me toward being normal. When I realized that most Christians don't play it dangerous, there was (and still is) a temptation to fall in line, to play it safe, to value comfort and conformity over the craziness of truly following God and his calling on my life.

It hasn't been easy for me, and I doubt it will be easy for you. But it is what will allow us to truly follow Jesus. It is what will lead to the life we've been longing for.

> We want to live sacrificial lives, but we tend to be selfish creatures.
> We want to live deep lives, but more often we find ourselves skimming life's surface.
> We want beautiful lives, but there's a lot of ugliness inside of us.
> We want holy lives, but we're pretty sinful.
> We want adventurous lives, but we're too apathetic.

It's tough.

But you can picture something different, can't you? Can you picture . . .

> The coffee shop barista who, through listening and caring and loving, becomes something of a pastor to the unchurched people with whom he works?
> The well-to-do family who downsizes their life so they can give 51 percent of their income to God and his kingdom, and finally discover the joy their money never bought them?
> The kid who inspires the other college students in the hall of his dorm to go with him on Saturday mornings to hang out with and feed the homeless?
> The family who starts their own little "bus ministry," stuffing kids from the neighborhood into their van to bring them to church each Sunday?
> The elderly widow who decides to become a "grandma" to the girls at a strip club so she can show them the love of God?
> The businessman who leaves it all behind to move to a third world country to serve the poor?
> The soccer mom who decides to live beyond herself and become the relational glue for the families on her kid's team,

and eventually leads every family to become a part of her church?

The teenager who goes without lunch during the school year so she can send $38 a month to sponsor a hungry child in Somalia?

The . . . *you*, living the life you long for, the life God has in mind for you, the life that may seem to be but is *not* beyond your reach?

So how can we leave our old lives behind to try something dangerous and different? How can we walk away from the beaten path and toward really living?

Let's find out.

3

Overcome the Bad Start

The following is a true story.

I apologize in advance.

Driving to a first date—especially a blind date—will always make a person nervous, and it may have been the nerves that caused the gurgling in his stomach. Whatever the cause, he felt like there was a tornado in his stomach. He prayed it wouldn't become a volcano.

Realizing he would have to go to the bathroom, he considered his options. He could stop and use a public restroom on the way, but then he would be late to her house. Not the first impression he hoped to create.

He could knock, introduce himself, and then ask to use the restroom. Again, not the best first impression. And his trampoline stomach led him to wonder how much time he might need in the bathroom. If he disappeared into the bathroom for an extended amount of time (not to mention the noises that might emanate from behind the locked door), he wouldn't just not get a second date, he would be mocked the next day on her Facebook page.

The best option, he realized, was to pick her up, drive to the restaurant, subtly excuse himself, and then *run* to the restroom. Hopefully she would be so absorbed in the menu she wouldn't notice how long he was gone.

He pulled up. Walked to the door. Knocked. She opened. Attractive. Nice smile. Introduced to roommate, who seemed sane. Sane friends are a good sign.

He wondered, *Can they hear my stomach? How can they not? I think I'm starting to sweat. Oh, I'm* really *sweating! I don't know if I can make it to the restaurant. I think I'm going to die.*

"I'm almost ready," she said, "just give me a minute."

He counted the seconds.

She said, "Okay, I'm ready."

She grabbed her jacket. They left the house. Walked to car. Stomach about to explode. *Open door for her? Polite, or too old-fashioned? Hmm, polite.* Door opened. She got in. He walked around car and got in. Stomach heaving like violent seas on *Deadliest Catch.* Started car. Drove down road. He tried to make small talk, but it was hard to concentrate enough to put together sentences and to speak out loud without groaning.

He realized, *I will* not *make it to the restaurant. There is no chance. I could stop at a gas station, but it would be weird to leave her sitting alone in my car. It's time to be honest.*

"I'm really sorry and really embarrassed," he apologized, "but I have to go to the bathroom. I'm just, uh, I'm just not feeling very well. I'm so sorry. Could we go back to your apartment real quick? And then we'll go to the restaurant."

She was, thankfully, sweet and understanding. "Sure, no problem."

He was relieved (and mortified) and did a quick U-turn.

They pulled up. He walked very quickly to her door, his legs pressed together as much as possible. He paused at the door. She finally caught up. Turned the knob.

Locked.

No, dear God, he prayed, *please get this door open fast!*

She apologized. "Sorry, let me find my keys." She searched through her pocketbook.

He died a little inside.

She searched through her pocketbook *again*.

Why Lord?! Don't you care about me? His excruciating intestinal pressure led him to question the existence of God.

She announced, "Wow, I forgot my keys." She assured him, "It's okay, my roommate will open the door."

She knocked.

No answer.

She knocked again.

He pounded the door and yelled, "Please! Hurry!"

No answer.

She said, "She doesn't seem to be here. Oh yeah, she did say she was about to go out. I apologize."

He considered his options. No. He was out of time, out of options.

He looked her in the eyes and said, "I am *so* sorry," ran into the yard, yanking his pants down as he ran, squatted, and then . . . the volcano erupted.

Right in the yard of his blind date.*

Sometimes relationships don't get off to a good start.

Your Start

Maybe your relationship with God didn't get off to a good start.

Honestly, I think a lot of people don't understand what the Christian life is all about when they start living it. And so many never *actually* live it. Some think the Christian life is about getting saved: *I put my faith in Jesus, and when the end comes I don't go to hell. That's what it's all about.*

Others think a relationship with God is about religion: *Just like basketball, there are certain rules and boundaries I need to*

---

*I know you're wondering, so to answer your question: no, I am not the guy in this story.

adhere to if I want to play the game of life correctly. Religion teaches me how to live in a way that is good and earns me good standing with God.

Still others think God is someone to know about. We learn about him. The really spiritual people become experts on the Bible: *The Christian life is an intellectual pursuit.*

A lot of people think of God as a cosmic vending machine: *He dispenses what I want if I'm faithful to him and order it up in prayer.*

A better, but still incomplete, version of what the Christian life is about pictures it as snuggling up on a couch with God: *The whole point of Jesus coming was so we could whisper sweet nothings to each other.*

And there are people who think it's just about serving the world: *Being a follower of Christ means I try to find old ladies to help across the street.*

If any of those are the idea you had starting out in your relationship with God, you got off to a bad start. And if you've continued to live out one of those ideas, no wonder you look at the Bible and think, *The life these people lived is* not *the life I'm living.*

No wonder you look at your own life and think, *There's no way this is the life Jesus died for me to live.*

It's no wonder you think something's wrong and there's got to be more.

But what is it?

The Christian life is about intimacy with God that leads to influence in the world.

Poured Into

The Christian life starts by being about intimacy with God. It's a relationship where God is not just a part of your life; he *is* your life. You get up in the morning and, realizing that the rest of your day there will be forces that drag you away from God, you pray for him to flood your heart. You pray desperately because you desperately want God, and you realize that on your own you're not capable of maintaining the level of passion for him you desire. It's the kind of intimacy that leads you to a simple goal for your life: each day you want to love God more than you did the day before. You have a prayer that subliminally becomes the soundtrack for your life: *God, pour yourself into me. God, pour yourself into me. God, pour yourself into me.*

You may be thinking that this isn't the way most people approach Christianity. They don't have that level of intensity. They're not pursuing intimacy with God at a radical level, not begging God to fill them. That's okay; *they're wrong*. And just because they're wrong doesn't mean you have to be as well.

You know who was right? God. God was right when he said we need to love him with *all* our heart, *all* our soul, *all* our strength, and *all* our mind.[1] God was right when he said "you will find me only when you seek me with *all* your heart."[2] God was right when he said we have to serve him with all our heart.[3] God was right when he said we have to obey him with *all* our heart.[4] God was right when he said we have to praise him with *all* our heart.[5] God was right when he said he would test us to determine if we truly love him with *all* our heart and soul.[6]

God really likes the word *all*.

I'm not so fond of it.* It's just very extreme. I prefer *some*. If God tells me to love him with *some* of my heart, I'm on it. Seek him with *some* of my heart? I can do that. Serve him with *some* of my heart? Consider it done.

But God doesn't want *some*. It's what most of us give him, but he's not interested. God wants *all*.

That's not easy for me. I have to fight for *all*. But I do fight for it, because I'm not willing to settle for less than God's best, and I'm not willing to live a cheap imitation of life. So I've built things into my life to move me toward *all*.

---

*Except when it comes to buffets. I want *all*-you-can-eat, not *some*-of-what-you-can-eat.

Every day, the first thing I do is read the Bible, because I realize the first thing I do will set the tone for the rest of my day. So before I go to sleep each night, I open the chapter I want to read the next day on the Bible app on my cell phone. When my eyes open in the morning, I grab my phone and read that chapter twice.

When I get out of bed, the first thing I do is get on my knees and ask God to start a revival in my heart. He knows that I want to spark a revival in my family, in my church, and in my city, but I know that I can't unless the revival starts in my own heart. I pray that God will flood into me and do something dramatic inside me. I tell him I want to love him more today than I did yesterday.

Then I run. I jog for about thirty minutes and listen to worship music. I've got a playlist of upbeat worship songs, another of contemplative worship songs, and another of my favorite worship songs. So I run and I listen to words that draw my heart to God's, and if you see me running down the street you'll see me huffing, puffing, and singing.

On my run, I hold a laminated card in my hand. On one side is a list of people I want to pray for every day. On the other is a description of the person I want to be for God. I'm not there yet (not even close), but I believe by reading it every day and praying for it to become reality, I'll keep moving closer.

When I finish running I usually take some time to pray and write in my journal. I try to share with God how I'm feeling about things and present my requests to him.

After a shower, I do our family Bible study with my wife and kids. We read a chapter together (the same chapter I read on my phone earlier that morning) and talk about how it applies to our lives.

Throughout the day I have my phone alarm set to go off every hour with different worship songs. I use those as reminders to keep my mind focused on God and on living in his presence. The different songs trigger different things I want to pray about: asking God to help me see that Jesus is enough for me, asking

God to use me to turn the world upside down, asking God to draw my heart back to his.

Reading all that you may think, *Well, aren't you special.* But I'm not. I don't do all that because I'm special. I do it because I'm *not.* I don't do it because I'm so holy and close to God. I do it because I'm *not.* And without all that, I know I won't experience *all* with him. I won't experience the intimacy with him that I was made for and that I long for.

And without intimacy with him, I won't have influence in this world. My life will have been a waste of space, a useless use of the world's supply of oxygen.

Poured Out For

The Christian life is about intimacy with God *that leads to influence in the world.* When you become a Christian it's very easy to be selfish about it. It may be the way we're taught about Christianity. ("Say yes to Jesus and God will give you an easy life! You can fix all your problems in three simple steps! God will bless you in every way you ask! What? You want a pony? God can give you a pony!") Or it may be that our lives are so jacked up that we almost require some time to be selfish—to really allow God to pour into us and bring the healing and wholeness we desperately need. But over time, as God continues to pour into you, your attitude eventually changes. You realize there's more; it's not all about you.

When you finally have real intimacy with God, you wouldn't dream of being selfish with it. You need everyone to experience it. In fact, you realize that if your intimacy with God doesn't connect you to other people and connect those other people to God, then really it's just an isolated and narcissistic act. But when you have a true passion for God, it automatically translates into a compassion for people. You can't stand the sight of injustice or human suffering or lost children without their heavenly Father. Those feelings aren't natural for you; they were planted deep in your heart when God came pouring in. Those feelings aren't natural for you, but they start to drive you. They lead you to see the world as God does, to dream big, impossible dreams, and to daily seek out ways you can become a force for good in this world God made and loves. And so you have a second song on your subliminal soundtrack: *God, pour me out for others. God, pour me out for others. God, pour me out for others.*

Again, you may be thinking that this isn't the way most people approach Christianity. They're not seeking to turn the world upside down. I mean, sure, some will find some way to serve in their church. But there's that word again—some. The word we like, but God's not so into. God is looking for *all*—all of ourselves living in intimacy with him, and all of ourselves living to influence others.

In fact, influence is the point of intimacy. Yes, God loves us and wants a deep abiding relationship with us that's unlike any other relationship we have. He wants intimacy with us, but intimacy is not the end. Serving the world; being light in darkness; bringing God's healing, compassion, justice, mercy, and truth; saving the world—*that's* the end.[7]

We are to have intimacy with God, but it's an intimacy that goes somewhere. That's what the Bible teaches.

In the Old Testament, Micah 6:8 says, "And what does the LORD require of you? To act justly and to love mercy and to walk humbly with your God." One of the three things God requires *is* about our relationship with him, but the other two point us toward action for people. Love for God leads to a life of promoting justice and showing compassion.

Jesus teaches us what will happen on judgment day when he splits the people who are destined to spend eternity with God from those who must be separated from him. What's the dividing factor? Jesus doesn't say to those who get in, "For I wanted to whisper sweet nothings with you and you came close and whispered, I wanted to snuggle and you told me you could be the big spoon or the little spoon, I wanted to know your secrets and you shared them with me." No. He says, "For I was hungry and you gave me something to eat, I was thirsty and you gave me something to drink, I was a stranger and you invited me in, I needed clothes and you clothed me, I was sick and you looked after me, I was in prison and you came to visit me."[8]

People will realize that, yes, they had to be saved from their sin by accepting Jesus as their rescuer, and, yes, they were supposed to have an intimate relationship with God, but no, that was *not* the end. The relationship was supposed to be for the world's sake.

And what were Jesus's last words before he went back to heaven? "Therefore go into your prayer closet and spend all your time with me, for I am with you always, to the very end of the age"? No, he said, "Therefore go and make disciples of all nations, baptizing them in the name of the Father and of the Son and of the Holy Spirit, and teaching them to obey everything I have commanded you. And surely I am with you always, to the very end of the age."[9] He is "with you"—there is a deep, close relationship—but the reason he gives that assurance is because he is sending you out into the world.

The more intimate our relationship with God, the more we're filled with love, compassion, and mercy for people, which lead us to serve selflessly and benefit the world.

It's critical that we understand the connection.

Intimacy *leads to* influence.[10]

Intimacy without influence is insular.

Influence without intimacy is impotent.

We need God pouring into us so we can be poured out for others. Without intimacy with God, we have little (if anything) to give.

Restart

The Christian life is about intimacy with God *that leads to influence in the world*. You may not have started out your relationship with God understanding that. It's possible you didn't really understand what the Christian life was about when you started living it. It's even possible that you've *never* really lived it.

But there's good news: even relationships that start badly can become great. In fact, remember the guy and girl at the beginning of this chapter whose blind date got off to such an atrociously bad start? Today they are happily married.

GOING ROGUE:

Your Renegade Assignment . . .
Should You Choose to Accept It

What's important is not enjoying this book but applying it—not learning about the renegade life but living it. And maybe you need a push in that direction, so consider this assignment your first gentle kick in the . . . well, you know. This first time we're going to focus on your relationship with God.

What was your understanding of the Christian life when you started living it?

Do you think it's possible you've been missing out on living the Christian life due to misunderstanding it?

God wants *all*. Create a plan (with a daily, weekly, monthly, and annual rhythm) that will allow God to pour into you. (What will you do every day? When will you do it? Every week? . . .)

Intimacy leads to influence. Take a prayerful look at yourself (your gifts, passions, personality) and start to dream a little: How could you pour yourself out for others in a way that would make a real difference for God?

4

Search in the Right Parking Garage

My life can get a little crazy sometimes. I'm a pastor of a church in the middle of Las Vegas. We have services on Sunday mornings *and* Monday nights. We put on an annual pastors' conference. I teach four courses a year in something our church calls "Verve University." I also speak at several other churches and a few conventions around the country each year. I write some books. I coach a few church planters over the phone. I've got a family and my son's baseball and football games and my daughter's piano lessons and school plays.

So my life can get crazy, and I can be thinking about so many things at once that I kind of lose my focus. I was invited to a pastors' "conversation" (more than a meeting, less than a convention) a few months ago. It was in Los Angeles from Monday morning to Wednesday afternoon. Because of our Monday night service, I had to miss the first day. I left from Vegas on Monday night, arriving at the hotel at 1:00 in the morning. The next day I had a one-hour coaching call from 8:00 to 9:00, which was perfect because the "conversation" didn't start until 9:00. In the middle of my call I went out to my car, put the address of the meeting location in my GPS, drove out of the parking lot, around the corner . . . and immediately into a parking garage. I realized I could have just walked from my hotel, but I didn't have time to drive back and then walk over, so I parked and walked to the meeting.

At the end of the day I was talking to the guy whose office we had all met in, explaining to him how I had driven about a tenth of a mile from the hotel to the parking garage. We laughed as he walked me out of the office building, at which point he pointed to a parking garage and said, "Well, that's where you're parked. See ya tomorrow!"

I went over to the parking garage and realized that I wasn't sure what floor my car was on. I had been in the middle of my phone call when I parked and hadn't been paying attention. I visualized my morning drive and determined it must be on the third floor. I walked around the third floor, but my car wasn't there. It was a massive parking garage, so I looked some more, but no luck. I decided it might have been the fourth floor, so I went up. No car. I went down to the second floor. No car. I had now spent over thirty minutes in a fruitless search in a hot parking garage, and I was starting to panic. I called my wife.

"I'm in trouble. I can't find my car . . . No, you don't understand . . . Yeah, I know it's got to be here, but I've looked every . . . No, you don't understand, it's not here . . . Yes, of course I'll keep looking, but I really don't think I'm ever going to find it."

I walked the third floor *again*, then the fourth *again*, and then the second *again*. Another half hour in the hot garage. My frustration started to mix with dehydration. I called my wife again.

"I'm in *big* trouble. I really can't find the car. I think you need to come get me . . . What? Yes, I know it's four hours each way, but what am I supposed to do, walk home? . . . Huh? Yes, I guess we WILL just lose the car forever. I can't think of any other solutions. . . . What's that?"

39

My wife encouraged me to find someone who worked at the garage; maybe they had some kind of video surveillance system that could help. I found a lady who told me she'd have a security guard come pick me up and drive me around to continue the search.

He pulled up in his golf cart and I jumped in, saying, "I'm so sorry," and "Does this happen a lot?" and "You're not going to tell people about this, are you?"

He told me not to worry and asked, "There are a lot of entrances to this garage. Which one did you come in?"

"Well, I have no idea. You see, my life gets kind of crazy sometimes . . ."

"Okay," he cut me off. "Think about this: When you walked out of the parking structure this morning, what did you see?"

This time I had an answer. "Restaurants!"

"That's weird." He looked confused. "Okay, what floor do you think it was on?"

We drove the third floor, then the fourth, then the second. Then, just in case, we drove the fifth, and then the first. Then we drove the third (again), then the fourth (again), then the second (again).

We drove for about an hour.

I had now spent nearly *two hours* searching for my car.

Finally, after a thousand apologies from me and a couple dozen, "I don't get this" from him, he asked, "Tell me again, what did you see when you walked out?"

"Restaurants."

"See, that's just weird," he responded, "because there are no restaurants next to us. But there are a couple outside the parking garage on the *other* side of the office building."

"In the other WHAT?" I asked.

"The other parking garage."

"There's another parking garage?" I was trying not to yell.

"Yeah. Wait, do you think you might have parked in that one?"

I walked to the other parking garage, went to the third floor, and immediately found my car.

Honestly I was so relieved, it didn't occur to me to feel stupid. And now I'm grateful for the experience because it's such a great metaphor for the trouble we can get ourselves into.

I think *we've* been searching in the wrong parking garage.

We're searching for life, life from and with God, but we've been searching (along with almost everyone else) in the wrong place. Maybe it's time for us to rebel against normal, against the tried but not so true.

What's It All About?

We think our relationship with God is all about *growth*, don't we? That's what everyone talks about. "Are you growing spiritually?" "I don't feel like I'm growing as a person." "My relationship with God isn't growing." "I want to find a church that can help me grow."

The problem is, this kind of thinking leads us to a selfish version of Christianity and leaves us feeling empty and wondering what we're missing.

The question is not "How do I grow?" When you think about it, that's actually a self-indulgent question, and God's plan for our lives has never been about self-indulgence.

It's about *love*.

Jesus said the two greatest things are loving God and loving people.[1]

The Cracker Jack surprise is that loving God and loving people happen to be what cause us to grow. But growth isn't really the point—love is.

Making it about growth is like the parents of a bride asking her groom, just before the wedding, "So, you really love our daughter?" and the groom replying, "Well, this isn't really about love for me. I mean, sure I love her, but this is about my growth. I just really want to grow. And I feel like I'll be a better person if I'm married. I'll be tempted less. I'll be more personally fulfilled. And I'm hoping being married improves my financial situation."

No. Growth isn't the point of marriage. Love is. Now it may be true that I grow as the result of marriage. I may be a better person, battle temptation more effectively, and be more fulfilled. But if I get married for those reasons, I am selfish and something is wrong. I've missed the point.

In the same way, becoming a Christian—*living* as a Christian—should cause me to grow, but that's not the point. The point is love—loving God and loving people.

When we make it about growth, we live self-indulgent and boring lives.

When we make it about love, we live selfless and adventurous lives.

The Beverly Hills Prison Nun

La Mesa prison in Tijuana is home to six thousand of Mexico's worst criminals and one eighty-plus-year-old nun, a nun who spends her days praying and counseling hardened murderers, gang leaders, and drug lords. She also fights for their rights. She makes sure they have medicine and clean water. The prisoners love her and call her Mother Antonia. She calls them her sons. The prison warden, Francisco Jiminez, says, "Mother Antonia brings hope to men and women here. And they find hope themselves. She spreads the love of God."[2] At the end of each day, Mother Antonia doesn't go home, because for over thirty years she has made a tiny cell in the prison her home.

Before moving into the prison in 1977, Mother Antonia was Mary Brenner Clarke, and she lived in luxurious Beverly Hills. But her intimacy with God transformed her life and led to a driving compassion for the broken and hurting. She felt that God called her to love the prisoners of La Mesa. And, as Jesus showed us, love shows up in person. Love reaches out. Love moves in. So that's exactly what Mary Brenner Clarke did.

Mother Antonia's presence led to a dramatic transformation in the prison, but still it was a dangerous place. At one point a riot broke out when she wasn't there. Eighty-two-year-old Mother Antonia returned to the prison that night to discover that soldiers were surrounding it, doing their best to contain the violence. The prisoners had taken hostages, fires had broken out, and bullets were flying. Mother Antonia told the police, "Let me go in, I know I can do something to stop the violence." They refused her request, explaining that they feared for her safety. "I'm not afraid," she told them. "When you love, you don't have anything to be afraid of. Love casts out fear, the Bible tells us, and I love the men there. . . . I can go into the cells and see the men, pray for them, bring them hope. . . . That doesn't mean I'm in accord with them. That doesn't mean I'm not going to show them what's wrong and try to calm something down. It just doesn't stop me from loving them." They gave her permission to go in.

Mother Antonia walked into the dark prison and found an influential inmate named Blackie. She told him, "It's not right that you're locked up here, hungry and thirsty. We can take care of those things, but this isn't the way to do it. I will help you make it better. But first you have to give me the guns. I beg you to put down your weapons."

Blackie told her, "Mother, as soon as we heard your voice we dropped the guns out of the window."[3]

A pastor said of Mother Antonia, "She's a walking gift of love."[4]

Loving God and loving others turns us into walking gifts of love to the world.

It's not about growth.

It's about love. God pours himself, his love, into us, and then we pour ourselves, God's love, out of us and into others.

But there's a problem.

This life God calls us to live, that we all long to live, often involves risk. Intimacy leads to influence, but there's usually danger stuffed into the middle of that equation like the cream filling of a Twinkie.

43

It may be risky to do what it takes to truly have intimacy with God. It will almost certainly be risky to do what it takes to truly have influence in this world. That's part of the reason it's a life most refuse to enter into. It's only for people who wear big boy pants, for those who are willing to live on the lunatic fringe. It's a risk-taking life that only renegades will choose.

PART 2

THE ANATOMY
OF RISK

Now that we've decided we need to be renegades, we have to figure out what will hold us back.

In this section you will learn some life-changing lessons. You'll see that God calls us to a risk-taking faith, but aversion to risk keeps us from living the renegade life. You'll understand the tension that often keeps us from taking risks, and learn the secret to overcoming fear. You'll be inspired by the faith of people in the Bible and today, and will be led to take some risks of your own.

You'll also meet some Christian ladies who spend their nights in Las Vegas strip clubs and see an old man hurtling through the sky because he wanted to illustrate trust in God. So hold on and keep reading.

5

You Can't Have Faith
without Risk

Since our kids were born, my wife, Jen, has been a stay-at-home mom and occasionally a part-time administrative assistant for a couple of businesses. But in the last few years something has grabbed her attention and won't let go. That something is sex slavery. She discovered there are more slaves today than at any other point in human history. She learned that the most common form of slavery involves young girls who are kidnapped and then forced to have sex with dozens of men every day.

But what could she do? Some people involved in this work execute daring rescues. My wife isn't that type. But when these girls are rescued they have to go through serious counseling to heal from the trauma they've experienced. My wife *is* that type. And so she prayed about it. To become a counselor would mean going back to college to get her master's degree. She'd been out of college for seventeen years. Back then she typed her papers on a word processor.* Also, we would need to take out about $30,000 in school loans. Did I mention we had just moved to Las Vegas to start a new church? Starting a new church does not put a family into a good financial situation. We were trying to figure out how we could ever possibly help our kids pay for their college, so to add another round of college tuition and school loans to the mix? It was a disconcerting thought. And though there are places of recovery and counseling in the United States, most of these girls are in countries like Cambodia. So what if Jen started down this path and it eventually led us to move to a third world country we had no interest in living in?

All told, as Jen considered what she felt God calling her to, she realized there was something holding her back. Risk.

So why don't you and I live in intimacy with God? And why don't we let that lead us to influence the world? On the surface, living this way seems so simple, even pleasant and enjoyable, but most people never experience intimacy with God in a significant way. Why?

Risk.

It's rarely easy. Intimacy with God leads to influence in the world. But there's almost always danger bubbling in that pot.

For some it may be intimidating to move toward intimacy with God. It is for me. I've been diagnosed as having attachment disorder. That means I view *intimacy* as a four-letter word. It means my favorite person to hang out with is me, and I can count on no fingers the number of people I find easy to trust. So intimacy with God? Scary.

It's intimidating to let God move you toward influence in the world, because what God asks us to do almost always pulls us outside our comfort zone. In fact, it often pulls us right into the crap-your-pants zone.

We love to play it safe, but God is not a safe God and Jesus never called anyone to live in safety. Jesus challenged people to follow him on a dangerous adventure, and he'll ask the same of us.

*If you're younger than thirty, you may want to take a minute and google "word processor." While you're at it, google "typewriters." You'll have some good laughs.

What Is Faith?

Think about this: What is it that gets you "into" Christianity? Faith, right? Place your faith in God, and Jesus leads you into becoming a Christian.

What is faith?

I know what you're thinking. Something like, *Faith is believing that Jesus is the Son of God, come to earth to . . .* And that's the nice Sunday school answer you're supposed to give, so congratulations. But is that *really* what faith is?

Think of it this way: let's say you're on a roof, twenty feet above the ground. I am standing on the ground below you. I shout, "Jump! I'll catch you. You can put your faith in me!"

What would it take for you to jump?

Faith.

But in that context, what is faith? Yes, it is belief in me, belief that I can catch you. But it's also *risk*. It would feel like risk, because it *would be* a risk. It would be a risk because you're being asked to put your faith in someone who may or may not be trustworthy.

Or what if your whole life, every time you've shared a secret, the person burned you by telling others. And now I say to you, "C'mon, share your secrets with me. You can trust me."

What would it take for you to tell me your secrets?

Faith.

But in that context, what is faith? Again, it is belief in me, belief that I won't violate your trust. But it is also risk. It would feel like risk, because it *would be* a risk. It would be a risk because you're being asked to put your faith in something.

Faith *is* risk. That's what faith is. It's what faith feels like.

You Cannot Play It Safe and Please God

What God is looking for is faith, and therefore God is looking for risk-takers. The Bible tells us in Hebrews 11:6, "And without faith it is impossible to please God." The idea: you cannot play it safe and please God.

Hebrews 11 lists people who are commended for their faith; their faith is *always* associated with action, and that action is *always* dangerous. In fact, that list wraps up like this:

> And what more shall I say? I do not have time to tell about Gideon, Barak, Samson and Jephthah, about David and Samuel and the prophets, who through faith conquered kingdoms, administered justice, and gained what was promised; who shut the mouths of lions, quenched the fury of the flames, and escaped the edge of the sword; whose weakness was turned to strength; and who became powerful in battle and routed foreign armies. Women received back their dead, raised to life again. There were others who were tortured, refusing to be released, so that they might gain an even better resurrection. Some faced jeers and flogging, and even chains and imprisonment. They were put to death by stoning; they were sawed in two; they were killed by the sword. They went about in sheepskins and goatskins, destitute, persecuted and mistreated—the world was not worthy of them. They wandered in deserts and mountains, living in caves and in holes in the ground.
>
> These were all commended for their faith, yet none of them received what had been promised.[1]

Does any of that sound safe to you?

Jesus once told a story about a master who, before he goes on a journey, entrusts varying amounts of money to three servants. While he's gone, the first two decide to invest his money, taking the risk that they may lose it all, but hoping they'll have more to give him upon his return. The third servant realizes that it's not his money, and therefore he shouldn't take any chances with it. He buries it so he's assured of having the full amount to give back to the master.

If you have never read that story in the Bible, who would you say did the right thing? The third guy! Instead of gambling with someone else's money, he does the right thing by playing it safe.

But when the master returns he commends the first two and condemns the third guy, calling him wicked and lazy.[2]

The point of the story? You cannot play it safe and please God.

The problem is that we love to play it safe. We want to minimize risk and have some assurance of success and a sense of peace about what we're going to do. And all of that sounds good and gives you nice, warm, fuzzy feelings inside, but it's not a life of faith, and it leads us away from adventure. Faith *is* risk. Faith stares down fear and embraces danger. God is not calling us to a safe place. He's calling us to the lunatic fringe.

Jesus didn't die to make us safe; he died so that we might die to ourselves, so he could take us where only dead men dare to go, where the living are too afraid to enter.

Jesus didn't die to make us safe; he died to make us dangerous.[3]

When we give our lives to Jesus, we lose our lives—which means we have nothing left to lose.

I recently read about missionaries in Africa who wanted to reach some slaves on an island just off the coast, but there was no way. Well, there was *one* way. The missionaries could connect with them if they too were slaves on the island. And so that's what they became. They sold themselves into slavery. What? That just doesn't make sense—*unless* you have no life left to lose. Unless you died with Christ, and the life you live is now for him.[4] When that's true, you live beyond fear and are free to risk. You become dangerous.

Faith Means Taking On the Giant

Think through the Bible. God often spoke to people, calling them to a specific task. Where in the Bible do you see God giving someone an easy assignment? Where in the Bible do you see God steering someone toward safety? Where in the Bible do you see someone following God's will without taking a great risk?

Never.

Abraham left everything and went to a land he didn't know. Noah built a giant boat with no sign of rain. Moses confronted Pharaoh. Elijah confronted the king. Gideon led the troops against a massive army. Rahab put her life in jeopardy by hiding the spies. Mary ruined her reputation by becoming an unwed mother. John

51

the Baptist was thrown in jail for speaking an unpopular message. Peter, John, and Paul were persecuted for talking about Jesus.

Or what about David? We love to hear the comic strip version of the little kid who took on the giant, but Goliath was a *huge* warrior of a man. He was so intimidating that every trained, armed Israelite soldier would not even consider fighting him. Why? Because they knew it meant death, and they had no intention of dying that day. Their agenda was safety. Who can blame them? Goliath was a killing machine, and they weren't stupid.

So David showed up. We don't know exactly how old he was, but he was probably just hitting puberty. He saw the Israelite army. They were his heroes. They were the older guys, the bigger guys, the stronger guys. The guys who have been trained to fight, trained to use weapons. On the other side of the valley he saw the Philistine army. But in the middle of the valley a man stood alone—the biggest man he'd ever seen. Freakishly big. Then he heard what the man was saying. He was screaming obscenities at the Israelites. He was mocking their God. Finally, David understood. This man was challenging an Israelite, any Israelite, to come out and fight him. But no one dared. They were playing it safe.

We know the story. David decided to face the giant, to fight for God. But don't make it a cartoon. David didn't smile and wink and say, "I'll be right back after I whip him up real good." David had to have experienced the same fear as every other Israelite. It was the same risk for him as for everyone else. It would have felt like a risk, because it *was*. He acted in faith, faith that God would defeat Goliath through him, and faith *is* risk. While everyone else played it safe, David played it dangerous. He was a renegade. And of all the Israelites who were there, he's the one who really lived that day, and the only one we still talk about.

Faith Means Quitting Your Job

I have a friend named Dallas.[5] When Dallas first walked into the church I started in Virginia Beach, he was about as far from God as a person could be. But Dallas kept coming and began to understand who Jesus was, and when you see Jesus for who he is, you can't help but want to follow him. And Dallas did.

About a year later we had a church service dedicated to God's call for us to love and care for the poor. At the end of the service we explained that the greatest need of homeless people was shoes, and we asked everyone to take off the shoes they were wearing so we could give them to someone who needed them more. Dallas and his wife, Anne, were two of the hundreds of people who left their shoes that day.

They went home and talked with their two teenagers about how giving their shoes was cool, but maybe not enough. Together they decided to make bologna sandwiches and go down to the beach and find homeless people to give them to. After that night they decided to give out bologna sandwiches to the homeless every Sunday. Soon the homeless realized that a bologna sandwich–wielding couple were roaming the beach, and so it was no longer Dallas and Anne who were looking for the homeless, it was the homeless who were looking for them. Eventually Dallas told his new homeless friends to meet him at a park near the beach at 5:00 each Sunday. About a hundred homeless people started gathering and waiting for Dallas. Soon Dallas enlisted the help of some friends from our church, and what they could offer went from bologna sandwiches to hygiene products, clothes, tents, blankets, medical care, counseling, and Bible studies.

At the time, Dallas worked in upper management for General Electric. But as the homeless ministry grew, it required more and more of Dallas's attention. One day Dallas met with me and told me he was quitting his job.

"What job did you get?" I asked.

Dallas explained that he wasn't quitting his job for another job. He was quitting his job for *no* job. He had decided to give his life to the ministry. He wanted to put all his available hours into loving and caring for the homeless.

"What will you do for money?" I asked.

Dallas reminded me that his wife had a job. I reminded him that his wife made about one-fourth what he did, so they would be reducing their income by more than 75 percent. How would they make it?

Dallas said they had done the math and created a new budget they'd have to get by on. It was a budget that didn't remotely resemble the one they had been living on for years. Soon they sold their really nice big house and moved into a really run-down little house.

We love to hear stories like that. We smile and talk about how inspiring it is. But think about it: Typically we try to avoid homeless people, so what must it have been like for Dallas and Anne to go down to the beach that first time *looking for* homeless people? And why were they the only ones in our church who thought to do that? Their family wasn't any less busy than other families with teenagers, so what did it feel like to commit *every* Sunday night to being with the homeless? When Dallas first thought of quitting his job, when they discussed living on a quarter of their current income, how did that feel? How would it feel to *you*? Many of us are working toward owning a newer, nicer home, so how do you think it felt to voluntarily move into an older, smaller one? I bet it all felt like risk. Because it was. Dallas was acting in faith, and faith *is* risk. While we were all playing it safe, Dallas played it dangerous. He was a renegade. Of the people I know in Virginia Beach, he's one of the few really living, and the one I'm writing about today.

If we want to really live, if we want an adventure worth talking about, we must live a life of faith. If we claim to have faith, but there's no risk involved, it's probably not faith.

And, by the way, faith can also mean going back to college. Pray for my wife: she's in her second year of graduate school, moving steadily toward becoming a counselor for girls who get rescued out of sex slavery. And pray that we can repay all her school loans. And that we don't end up moving to Cambodia.

6

Stare Down the Risk

What did you do when you were nineteen years old? I studied to get good grades in college, played fantasy football, fought a lot with my girlfriend, and played video games. Katie Davis moved to Uganda.

She had visited the year before, as an eighteen-year-old, and upon returning home couldn't get the people in Uganda out of her mind. So in the summer of 2007 she moved there to teach kindergarten at an orphanage. She immediately learned that most of the kids in her area couldn't afford to pay the school fees, and so they had no chance at an education. Katie started a child sponsorship program, quickly getting 150 children from her orphanage sponsored so they could go to school, eat three hot meals a day, and receive medical care.

Soon Katie established a nonprofit organization called Amazima Ministries International to meet the physical, emotional, and spiritual needs of the people in Uganda.

She then began building relationships with the Karimojong people, who were the poorest and most needy of all. She started a program in this community that provided food for over 1,600 children a day.

Next, Katie initiated a vocational program to empower women from the Karimojong tribe to start businesses and manage their money.

During this time Katie personally adopted thirteen Ugandan daughters.[1]

I don't know Katie Davis, but I can tell you something about her: she's just a person. Just like you. Just like me. And I can tell you that none of this was easy for her. There had to be fear with every new step. Yes, it's a great story, but it's a story filled with risk.

In fact, nothing great ever happens without us stepping firmly outside our comfort zone.

Right?

Trying out for the team, taking the last-second shot, going to college, starting a new job, launching a new product or company, getting married, having a baby, going on a mission trip or becoming a missionary, starting a Bible study or a ministry or a church—everything that has potential for producing greatness requires risk.

There's a problem: risk induces fear. Not always to the same degree, but risk *always* induces fear.

The Secret

There's a secret to overcoming fear. Whether or not you take a risk is generally based on the amount of fear it induces, but if you learn this secret it can change your life by giving you the courage to venture out where you normally wouldn't.

Here it is: your willingness to risk is based on potential return.

For instance: Would you run into a burning house? No, you wouldn't. Why? Because it's a risk, and the fear of taking that risk would be too great.

But let's change your focus: Would you run into a burning house if you realized your pet goldfish were inside? No, you still wouldn't. Why? Because it's a risk, and the fear of taking that risk is greater than the potential return of saving your goldfish.

But let's change your focus one more time: Would you run into a burning house if you realized your *child* were inside? Yes, you would. Why? It's the exact same risk and would induce the exact same fear, but you would do it because the return is worth the risk.[2]

The reason most Christians won't take the risks necessary to have influence in the world is because they are stopped by fear.

Why don't most Christians tithe? Because of the risk of living on only 90 percent of their salary.

Why don't most Christians volunteer? Because of the risk of being overwhelmed by the extra time commitment.

Why don't most Christians share their faith? Because of the risk of being rejected by their friends.

When we stare at the risk, we're stopped by our fear. But we can stare down the risk by staring at the potential return. Lives are changed forever when we're generous with our money, when we volunteer, and when we share our faith. It doesn't change the risk involved, but we can overcome our fear when we realize the return is worth the risk. In fact, when we calculate and focus on the potential return, we realize that it's a bigger risk *not* to tithe, *not* to volunteer, *not* to share our faith.

Your willingness to risk is based on potential return. The potential return of being a renegade for God, the return on leaving behind the way you've been living out your faith for a better way, the return on rising above what's normal and expected to attempt what's abnormal but extraordinary—it's worth the risk.

Think again about David. Do you think he *wanted* to fight Goliath? Do you think he woke up that morning hoping he might be able to take on a giant warrior who would likely literally tear him limb from limb?

No.

When David looked at Goliath, he saw battling him as the same risk every other Israelite saw. The thought of fighting him aroused the same fear in him as it did in everyone else. So why was David willing to do what no one else would?

Because he didn't stare at the risk, he stared at the potential return. In fact, the first sentence we hear David speak is, "What will be done for the man who kills this Philistine and removes this disgrace from Israel?"[3] David looked past the fear and saw the reward: defeating the blasphemous giant would glorify God and let the Philistines and Israelites know that he is deserving of honor.

Think again about Dallas. Do you think he *wanted* to have no income and leave his nice house? Do you think his life goals included not having enough money to take his family on a vacation or help pay for his kids' college?

No.

When Dallas had the idea of leaving everything to minister full-time to homeless people, the thought aroused the same fears in him as it would anyone else. So why was Dallas willing to do it?

Because he didn't stare at the risk, he stared at the potential return. I remember Dallas describing what the ministry would be like someday—addiction recovery groups, homeless men's prayer breakfasts, transition housing—all of it helping homeless people to get off the streets and into a life-changing relationship with God. Dallas looked past the fear and saw the reward: if Dallas and his family chose to live simply, others might be able to simply live. The sacrifice he was making and the time he would spend with the homeless would let them know that they had worth and significance. Perhaps they would become open to the idea that God could love them and provide a home for them in heaven.

And it's the same with Katie Davis. No nineteen-year-old moves to Uganda without thinking, *What am I doing? Am I crazy? What if this doesn't work?* But Katie looked past the fear and saw the reward: children would be released from poverty. Instead of growing up hungry on the streets, they would grow up filled with love in a Christian orphanage. They would have a godly role model and, hopefully, end up living a life worth living.

In the last chapter we checked out Hebrews 11:6, where we learned that it's impossible to please God without faith, and that risk is inherent in faith. I mentioned how Hebrews 11 has a hall of fame of those who lived by faith, and for each of these people, living by faith meant taking risk. In Hebrews 11:1, the Bible says, "Now faith is being sure of what we hope for and certain of what do not see." Acting on our faith is about what we *see*. It's about our ability to see the future, to see what's currently unseeable. It's about whether we're staring at the risk or the reward.

In Hebrews 11:6, after being taught that it's impossible to please God without faith, we're told that we must believe that God "rewards those who earnestly seek him." Living by faith is about looking ahead and seeing the results of our faith.

We're told that Abraham was willing to leave what he knew and go to an unknown new place because "he was *looking* forward to the city with foundations, whose architect and builder is God."[4] It was about what Abraham was looking at.

We're told that Moses confronted Pharaoh and led the Israelites out of slavery "because he *saw* him who is invisible."[5] In fact, describing all these faith legends, the Bible says, "All these people were still living by faith when they died. They did not receive the things promised; they only *saw* them and welcomed them from a distance."[6]

Living by faith (and remember faith *is* risk) is all about what you *see*. It's about looking past the fear and seeing the reward.

So what about you? I don't know what you did at nineteen, but what are you doing at _____ (insert your current age)? And what will you be doing at _____ (insert your current age plus one)? Are you going to continue doing what you've always done, or are you going to do something different? Are you going to continue with the tried and not so true, or are you willing to be a renegade? Are you open to the faith adventure God has for you?

Yes, it's scary.

But you can do it, if you know how.

You stare down the risk by staring at the potential return.

GOING ROGUE:

Your Renegade Assignment . . .
Should You Choose to Accept It

In this chapter we saw the amazing story of Katie Davis, who was such a renegade she moved to Uganda (at nineteen!) and ended up doing all kinds of things for poor and needy children, including adopting thirteen girls to be her own.

Question: What could you do for the poor or specifically for needy children? Perhaps you're not in a position where you could move to Uganda, but you could do something in your town.

Here it comes. You've just been presented with a risky idea, and so you're feeling . . . fear. The fear will naturally lead to excuses. "But I couldn't because . . ." "But you don't understand my situation . . ." "But how would I . . ."

Stare down the risk by staring at the potential return.

Get out a piece of paper and draw a line down the middle. Label the left side "Risk" and the right side "Potential Return."

In the left column write down two to four things you could do for poor or needy children. For instance: you could adopt a child. You could become a foster parent. You could sponsor a child through an organization like Katie's or Compassion International. Your family could volunteer every Saturday at a local homeless shelter.

In the right column write down the potential return. How might taking that risk pay off for the needy person/people you'd be helping? How could it change their lives? And how might it pay off for you? How might it change your life?

Then stare at the right column.

I mean it.

Literally.

Stare at the potential return. And ask God to enable you to see the future, to see what can't be seen, and to help you step out in faith to take the specific risk he's calling you to take.

And when you take that step, you'll have just moved closer to being a renegade.

7

Trust the Catcher

The key for anyone to overcome fear is to focus on the potential return, but those of us who follow Jesus have another factor that enables us to overcome fear: the catcher.

Henri Nouwen was a priest, professor, and author who, in his late sixties, went to see the Flying Rodleighs, a trapeze troupe who had become friends of his. As he sat in the audience, Nouwen realized that everyone in the crowd focused on the flyer—the person who flies through the air—and didn't pay attention to the catcher. But the flyer wouldn't dare take the risk without the assurance that he would be caught. It was really the catcher who allowed the fantastic to happen. Nouwen later received permission to try the trapeze himself. They put a harness on him, and the trapeze artist told Nouwen, "The flyer must never try to catch the catcher. He must wait in absolute trust. The catcher will catch him. But he must wait. His job is not to flail about in anxiety. In fact, if he does, it could kill him. His job is to be still. To wait."[1] Then this elderly scholar flew giggling through the air. After each fall into the net, he went up again and again. Knowing he was truly safe allowed him to take what would have otherwise looked like huge risks. He said,

> If we are to take risks, to be free, in the air, in life, we have to know there's a catcher. We have to know that when we come down from it all, we're going to be caught, we're going to be safe. The great hero is the least visible. Trust the catcher.[2]

Living in the Tension

Psychologists tell us that the two basic needs every person has are security and significance.[3] Security is a need to feel safe. Significance is a need to feel that your life matters.

Here's the problem: our two basic needs are generally at odds with each other. What it takes to make our lives significant often moves us out of our comfort zone, and can therefore threaten our sense of security. For instance:

If you find your security in the acceptance of others, what if the action you need to take to have significance will cause others to look down on you?

If I find security in success, what if what I need to do to have significance is leave the growing church I started to plant a new church in an area where there is little chance of success?

If Dallas found his security in having a good salary and nice house, what if what he needed to do to have significance was quit his job and sell his house to lead a homeless ministry?

If we find our security in feeling safe, what if what we need to do to have significance is fight a giant?

So what is the answer?

God is.

God calls us to a life of intimacy with him, which provides security, and to a life of influence in the world, which provides significance. If we do a relationship with God *right* and live life as he intends, both of our primary needs will be met.

The key is finding our security in him. God invites us repeatedly to make him our safe place.[4] And when he is where you find your security, you are freed to take great risks. What you're led to do may hurt your reputation, deplete your savings account, break your heart, reduce your salary, take away your popularity, lose you your boyfriend or girlfriend, or even make you homeless—but the one thing it *won't do* is separate you from God.[5] And so no matter how risky your life becomes, no matter how dangerous the places you're led to, you are always safe. Even if everyone is watching you, and you fall, you know there is a less-visible hero who will catch you.

Following God into a Strip Club

Several ladies in our church volunteer in a ministry to the strip clubs and brothels that fill and surround Las Vegas. Each week they go into strip clubs to build relationships with the girls who work there. They try to show them God's love in a practical way and then take those friendships outside the club and eventually to Jesus.

The ladies in this ministry are not former strippers. They're moms and housewives and teachers and salespeople. Strip clubs and brothels are as unfamiliar and uncomfortable to them as they would be to you. But they do it, and they're great at it.

Why do they do it? Because they feel like God called them to it. It's not easy.

There's fear. Several strip clubs they visit have had shootings in the parking lot. They end up in some uncomfortable situations. They worry about the girls' pimps. To them, the girls are precious human beings. To their pimps they are commodities, streams of income. Pimps don't like it when you mess with their money.

And they experience heartbreak as well. When Stacy was a young teenager, a guy from Las Vegas started contacting her through her MySpace page, encouraging her to come out and join him in Sin City. When Stacy turned eighteen, she moved to Vegas and her new "boyfriend" quickly introduced her to heroin and to working in strip clubs. A few months later her boyfriend shot her up, but something went wrong. Stacy wasn't responding. Her boyfriend carried her to his car, drove to the nearest hospital, pushed her out of the car, and drove away. Someone saw her and ran into the hospital to get help. Stacy was brought into the hospital and declared dead, but they managed to revive her. A few hours later, when she finally came around, they asked her whom she wanted to call. She wanted to call the ladies from the ministry who visited her strip club.

Soon a couple of ladies from our church who volunteer with the ministry showed up. They talked to Stacy about Jesus, and she seemed very receptive. The next day she was released from the hospital and came to our church service. She agreed to go to rehab, and so we feverishly worked to raise the money to send her. Pretty quickly we got it together, and Stacy went to rehab. She let us know that it was going great, that she loved it, that it was really helping. And then she walked out. After about a week she decided she'd had enough, left, and went back to her old life.

It's heartbreaking. And it's *not easy*.

So how are these ladies able to do it?

They know they're loved.

They're loved perfectly by a perfect Father, and perfect love casts out fear.[6]

God's love doesn't put us in a comfortable place where we can live free from risk; it prepares us for a dangerous place where we're free *to* risk.

These ladies are living that.

And you can too.

You just have to trust the catcher.

THE RENEGADE LIFE

You want to be a renegade. You now know how to overcome fear and take risks so you can actually live out real faith. But what does the renegade life look like?

In this section you'll meet a mother whose son was killed by a drunk driver, a missionary to a motorcycle gang and a tattoo shop, the highest-ranking female in a white supremacist hate group, and a crazy bunch of renegades, including a nurse, a car mechanic, and a former pimp. You'll hear about my invitation to do stand-up comedy at a nudist colony.

More importantly, you'll discover Jesus's mission for every Christian and his particular calling on your life, and you'll learn the secrets of how to engage in them effectively.

8

Get God in Your Gut

Elizabeth Morris sat up, waiting. She was tired, but she couldn't go to sleep until her son Ted came home. Ted was a college student home for Christmas break. Ted was late. Then Elizabeth received the phone call all parents fear: "Mrs. Morris, your son has been in an accident."

Tommy Pigage was from a broken home and had started drinking at an early age. Now twenty-four, he was well on his way to becoming a full-fledged alcoholic. He had been at a party with friends, who begged him not to drive. But Tommy refused their offers to take him home and staggered to his Buick. The last thing he remembers is approaching the Canton Street Bridge in Hopkinsville. That's where he blacked out. He never saw eighteen-year-old Ted Morris coming the other way in his AMC Hornet. Tommy's car crossed over the center line, and Ted died the next morning. Tommy's blood alcohol level was almost three times the amount required to be legally intoxicated.

A month later, Elizabeth and her husband attended the trial. Elizabeth admitted that she wanted Tommy dead. She was shocked when the grand jury reduced the murder charge to manslaughter, and furious when Tommy pleaded innocent. The trial was delayed, and delayed again, and then again. "Every time it would be delayed, I would get more upset, and my hatred for him would grow," Elizabeth said. Her anger only grew when, almost two years after the accident, the trial finally closed with Tommy changing his plea to guilty and being freed on probation.

Elizabeth wanted revenge. She would fantasize about driving down the road, seeing Tommy walking, and pinning him to a tree with her car then watching him die a slow, agonizing death. She spent a lot of her time tracking Tommy, hoping she would catch him violating his probation so he could be sent to prison.

There was only one problem.

Elizabeth Morris was a Christian. And as she brought her feelings to God, she came to the realization that her heavenly Father had also lost his only Son. On the cross Jesus had said, "Father, forgive them" about the soldiers who crucified him, and that in a very real sense *she* had put Jesus on the cross through her sins, but that God had forgiven her. And she realized that she had to forgive Tommy.[1] Though it made her uncomfortable, she couldn't escape it.

Compassion for Your Son's Killer

One day Elizabeth was driving past Tommy's house and saw him sitting on the front porch. She asked him to get in her car and told him she wanted to help him. But not long after that, Tommy violated his parole agreement by getting drunk and was sentenced to three months in prison. During his time in jail, Elizabeth was his most faithful visitor. After Tommy got out, the Morrises would drive him to the schools where as part of his probation he had to give lectures against drinking and driving. On the way home from one, Elizabeth's husband, Frank, talked to Tommy about Jesus. And at about 10:00 that night, Ted Morris's father baptized Ted Morris's killer into Christ.

The Morrises eventually unofficially adopted Tommy as their own son. Tommy now attends church with the Morrises. They take him out to eat every Sunday after the service. On Thursdays they sometimes go roller-skating together, and on weekends they often go bowling. Tommy calls them every day. Elizabeth says, "I would miss it if he didn't call."

My Favorite Word

In Matthew 9 we see Jesus heal a paralytic, a dead girl, a sick woman, and the blind and the mute. Jesus continued on his journey that day through various towns and villages. And the Bible says, "When he saw the crowds, he had compassion on them."[2] The word *compassion* is translated from a word in the original language of the passage. The word is *splagna*.

That is my favorite word.

Partly because of how it sounds. Say it out loud, but make it guttural. Force it to come from deep in your stomach.

"SPLAGNA!"

It sounds like the noise someone would make when they throw up, as in "Whoa, I am so sick. I just splagnaed all over the place."

And that also happens to be what it means.

Splagna refers to a person's intestines or bowels. The idea is of having your guts ripped out or your bowels removed. It's a feeling you get in your stomach, a deep, wrenching, painful feeling generally reserved for times of intense nausea and frantic running to the bathroom.

But we learn in this story from Jesus's life that it can also be a reaction to something you see. It's a feeling you get when you see something unacceptable, something you cannot tolerate that causes a visceral, painful reaction.

That's splagna, and that's what Jesus had when he saw the crowds.[3] Why did Jesus have splagna on them? The rest of that verse tells us: "He had compassion on them, because they were harassed and helpless, like sheep without a shepherd."[4] Jesus saw people who were experiencing injustice. He saw people who had no one to help them. And mostly what he saw were people who were like children without their heavenly Father, and he could not tolerate it; his insides started churning. It made him sick to his stomach. He had splagna.

CiCi

The reason intimacy with God leads to influence in the world is because when we allow God to pour himself into us, we receive his intestines. People talk about inviting God into our hearts, but I wonder if it would be more theologically accurate to invite him into your gut.

From an early age, CiCi was a member of "The Order" (aka Brüder Schweigen). The Order was a white supremacist, nationalist revolutionary organization probably best known for its role in the 1984 murder of radio talk show host Alan Berg, which inspired the movie *Talk Radio*. CiCi's childhood neighbor David Tate, one of the leaders of The Order, used her to smuggle drugs into the Missouri state prisons. As she got older her role became reading the typed speeches of the imprisoned David Lane (another leader in The Order) at skinhead meetings around the country. She also gathered untraceable guns and recruited as many people as possible for the revolution their "White Army" wanted to unleash on America. Friends with Timothy McVeigh and living in a home with walls covered with pictures of Hitler and swastikas, CiCi completely bought into the life.

CiCi got married for the first time at age fifteen to a drug dealer. She quickly became an addict, doing all kinds of drugs but mostly crystal meth. In her early days of addiction she would wait till the first of the month to beat her sister and take her child support check for drug money. CiCi watched her sister and her five kids get evicted—repeatedly—because she had stolen their only way to support themselves.

CiCi's first husband committed suicide, but she married again, and again, and again. In fact, CiCi has been married *eleven* times. Most of her husbands have been drug-dealing skinheads.

Whenever CiCi began to have misgivings about her involvement in The Order and tried to separate herself, her husbands would send orders from jail to have her beaten. She's been stabbed twice and shot fourteen times.

Finally CiCi had enough and decided to get away. She moved to Las Vegas because she heard that there were very few skinheads there due to the racial diversity of the city. In Vegas, CiCi continued to struggle with her drug addiction. One day she wanted to get high but instead called a friend. It was a woman CiCi used to do drugs with, but who had since given her life to God and cleaned up her act. This friend told CiCi to go to a certain motorcycle shop, ask for Kenny, and have him recommend a tattoo-friendly church. Kenny told her that he hadn't found one in Vegas. CiCi continued to struggle but then met a guy who told her about his church. His name was Warren. He was a fire-breathing clown and a former atheist.

Soon CiCi called us, explaining that she was a crystal meth addict whose husband had just had her beaten up and her apartment trashed. CiCi ended up coming to our church, encountering the radical love of God, and being radically transformed by it all.

This past Thanksgiving, CiCi got a few people from our church to help her feed homeless people dinner in a park. They fed 285 people. I asked CiCi what led her to do that, assuming that she had probably experienced homelessness at some point in her troubled journey. She told me she had briefly been homeless once, but that wasn't her reason for wanting to help the homeless. What's driving her is that the homeless are the skinheads' biggest targets. They practice killing on homeless people because no one misses them when they're gone; the police rarely investigate when one is found beaten to death. She says that now nothing gets to her like seeing a homeless person smile when she serves them.

Encountering God transformed her from a person who viewed the homeless as expendable to someone who views them as harassed and helpless, like sheep without a shepherd. It drove her to action. Intimacy with God led her to be an influence for the homeless.

You and I may not have as sordid a past as CiCi, but we do have a past. And in light of our sin, when we think about the grace of God that has flooded into our lives, we can't help but want to give that grace to others.

It's a heart filled with compassion that drives us to live a renegade life.

In the story from Matthew 9, Jesus had splagna for the crowds, so he turned to his disciples and said, "The harvest is plentiful but the workers are few. Ask the Lord of the harvest, therefore, to send out workers into his harvest field."[5] Jesus asked them to pray. To pray that God would find people who care about the harassed and helpless. To pray that God would find people who care that God has lost children here on earth who don't know him. To pray that those people would care enough to do something about it. To pray that those people would find ways to right injustice, to serve, and to reconnect those people to their heavenly Father.

And you and I, we get the honor of being the answer to Jesus's prayer.

Just like CiCi, and just like Elizabeth Morris.

And *that* is splagna.

Splagna leads us into the renegade life.

9

Discover Your Calling

The spark was lit when I decided to follow Jesus. I was on fire for God, and I wanted to be set ablaze. I couldn't wait to serve God, make a difference, change the world.

But I didn't really know how.

I was cultivating my relationship with God, and I understood the basics: spend time with him, love people, give, volunteer. I knew God had uniquely made me and had a unique calling on my life, but I felt like someone watching a new M. Night Shyamalan movie: I was clueless as to what my story was all about or where it was going.

As I mentioned, I began to realize that becoming an attorney wasn't what I was supposed to do with my life. I couldn't stop thinking about the elements that made up my story—my painful childhood, growing up without ever being told about Jesus, and never being invited to church. It burned in me, and I *had* to use my life to make sure others didn't go through the same thing I did. I couldn't stand the idea that there were others in the world like the old me.

I had to do something about it. I decided to go into ministry and transferred from law school to seminary. Considering my background, and who I was, it was a bizarre decision. It felt a bit like Lady Gaga becoming a librarian.* I wasn't sure what I would do in ministry. I knew only two things: I was passionate about helping people who were where I had been—far from God, broken, caught up in sin, and ignored by the church—and I would *not* be a preacher. I had seen a couple of preachers, and they were great men, but they were so different from me. These men grew up in Christian families, wore ties instead of T-shirts, and thought potlucks were better than ordering pizza. They even had the audacity to schedule church events for Sunday afternoon when football was on. Their wives could play the piano and make casseroles. I didn't have a wife, but piano playing and casserole-making weren't on the list of qualities I was looking for. Plus I was pretty sure they all drove the speed limit, and I didn't understand the words they used like "propitiation," "dispensation," "atonement," and "vestibule." And how did they promise to pray for everyone? I could never pray that much!

So I figured I wasn't a good fit for that job.

But the seminary I attended required a preaching class. It was a roomful of young white guys who wanted to be preachers plus three oddballs: me (a young white guy who *didn't* want to be a preacher), an old ex-hippie dude, and a middle-aged African-American man who was already a preacher at a big church in town but was getting his PhD.

We took turns preaching. Each class someone would present a sermon and the rest of the class offered critiques. When my day arrived, my non-piano-playing girlfriend Jen happened to be in town visiting, so she came to watch. I warned her this was my first time giving a sermon and preaching wasn't my thing, and I still wasn't sure what dispensation meant so I left that out of the sermon, and I was the only one in class who didn't want to make this a career. (For which she should have been thankful, because I still wasn't sure of her casserole-making skills.)

---

*Can you picture her sitting behind the desk in her meat dress, explaining the Dewey Decimal system to some terrorized children? "Make her take it off! Why does her hair look like that? What's wrong with her shoulders?! Waaaa!"

So I walked up to the podium thingy, gave my sermon, and waited for the criticism, but no one spoke for a minute or two. Thoughts starting going through my head, such as *Was it really that bad?* and *Why do you mock me with your silent stares?* and *Just say how bad it was; I don't need your approval!* and *I will burn this seminary to the ground!* When the African-American pastor spoke up, he said, "It's about time we got some black preaching in here! That's what I'm talking about—a white man with some soul!" Then the old ex-hippie dude chimed in, "Keep the devil off your back, man. Keep the devil off your back." And that was it.

As we walked out, Jen asked, "What did that man mean about you being a black preacher?" I gave her a blank look. "I have no idea, but I guess maybe he thought I was good?" She then asked, "Why did that old weird guy tell you to keep the devil off your back?" I shrugged. "I have no idea, but I think I saw him smoking some peyote before class."

That experience was the first of many clues that I was wrong: I *was* supposed to be a preacher.

The question I investigated every day at seminary was, "How can I use my life to help the most people who are far from God get close to God?" My studies led me to an unexpected answer: church planting. Starting new churches tends to be the most effective way to help lots of people find and follow Jesus. And so I decided to be a preacher . . . in a new church plant.

Eventually I decided to start a church. We believed God wanted us to do it, and so I prayed, asking God to show me exactly where, but I never felt any specific direction. So I researched and visited options, and eventually decided on Virginia Beach, Virginia. The plan was for it to be my one and only church plant, but after eleven years there, God spoke. This time his call was much more direct, and it was clear he was telling me to start another new church in Las Vegas, on or near the Strip. I was stunned, but the vision quickly came together in my head.

I wanted to reach people who were broken. Where are there more broken people than in Sin City? I felt as though I could connect with people who had never gone to or had rejected church. It turns out less than 9 percent of Vegas residents go to church, so about 1.8 million do not. And my father was a professional poker player and degenerate gambler who ruined his life in Las Vegas, so there was a cool redemptive story line to me ministering to hurting people in that city.

It took almost twenty years, but I think I'm now finally living fully in my calling. It's interesting to look back and see all the different ways I discovered my calling. Some of it came from a gut feeling birthed out of an anger burning inside me. I also deciphered my calling through the affirmation of others. For a time I also took a very intellectual approach. And later there was an almost mystical element where God spoke to me and made his specific calling on my life more clear.

I don't know how long it may take you, and I'm not sure what methods you'll need to employ, but it is important to discover the calling God has on your life. It is then vital to follow that calling in faith, realizing that faith will often carry us out of our comfort zone where we live for ourselves to a sometimes dangerous place of compassion where we live for others. And when you discover and start living out your calling, you'll feel like you're newly born, like you're breathing for the first time, finally understanding why you've been walking around the earth all these years. You'll enter into a partnership with God where you don't just believe in him, you *need* him, and you'll experience the thrill of being used by God to change the world.

For those reasons and more, you need to discover your calling. But how? Here are some ideas.

Discovery Method 1: Listening

Some people discover their calling by hearing God speak directly to them. Let's be honest: this is what everyone wants. It makes for a mystical and kind of romantic story: "I was walking on the beach, praying, when I heard God's voice and he told me I should devote my life to being a lifeguard. At just that moment I heard the cries of fourteen Guatemalan orphans who had all been trapped in the undertow. What they were doing in Myrtle Beach I'll probably never know. They were about fifty yards offshore, but I was able to swim back and forth fourteen times and save each one, and it was because the Lord was with me. That was the day when I began living out my calling." Or, "I always thought I should go into ministry, but one day I was driving down the road, praying, asking God what I should do with my life when suddenly the canned ham factory I was driving past exploded. My car was literally covered in canned ham. But I couldn't worry about that, because the factory was on fire. The smell of baking ham was everywhere, and people were trapped inside. I ran in and out of the factory repeatedly, saving several people (and what hams I could). That was the day God told me that being a firefighter was my true calling."

Who doesn't want one of those stories?

And you may get one. Pray and ask God how you should use your life for him. And listen. He may speak. He may tell you to devote your life to small children, to become a teacher and to volunteer in your church's children's ministry. Or he could call you to go overseas and become a missionary. Or you may hear his voice telling you to minister to the homeless people in your city.

So ask and listen, and God may speak, and hopefully you'll be listening.

But if that doesn't seem to work, if you don't feel like you hear directly from God, don't be discouraged, because there are other ways you can discover your calling.

Discovery Method 2: Your Past

Another way to discern what God wants you doing in the future is to examine your past. God doesn't want you to waste your experiences, so he may call you to minister in a way that takes advantage of them.

People sometimes don't get this. I've talked to a lot of people who are praying about leaving their careers and going into paid full-time ministry. I'll ask, "What have you been doing?" The person will perhaps explain that he has twenty years of experience in business and is now thinking of becoming a preacher. Well, that is an option. But is it possible that becoming an executive pastor at a large church, where a business background could prove invaluable, would be a wiser choice?

Your pain is also part of your past that God may use in creating a path for your future. This has been a critical aspect of my calling. I thought I wasn't preacher material because I didn't grow up in a Christian home and had a dysfunctional family, but actually it has set me up perfectly to speak to people with similar backgrounds. I had an abusive father. That experience, though I wouldn't wish it on anyone, has allowed me to really connect with people who have experienced abuse. I never went to church and no one ever told me about Jesus. My calling has been to start churches for people who aren't interested in church and to reach people who are very far from Christ or who may find more traditional churches intimidating.

What about you? Perhaps you lost a child and could start a support group for people carrying that same pain. Or maybe you were a lonely kid without any mentors, but you could turn that around and volunteer as a Big Brother or Big Sister. Maybe you were an athlete and have always gravitated to hitting, throwing, and bouncing balls, and God is calling you to start a sports ministry at your church, or to coach kids' teams in a way that brings the families involved to God.

Discovery Method 3: Favorite Movies

Here's a fun idea that might help you find your life's passion: name your three favorite movies, then examine those three movies to determine the common thread. That thread may reveal your passion in life. I learned this from leadership guru Michael Hyatt. His three favorites are *Star Wars*, *Lord of the Rings*, and

To Kill a Mockingbird. The thread? He says, "Outcasts who overcome their past to absolutely change the world."

My three favorites are *Silence of the Lambs*, *Nightmare on Elm Street*, and *Throw Momma from the Train*. So what do you learn? I am going to kill your mother while she sleeps!

I'm kidding. Really, my three favorite movies are probably *Hoosiers*, *Jerry Maguire*, and *Almost Famous*. The common thread? I'll figure that out. It's *my* thread and *my* calling. But what are *your* favorites? And what do they tell you about you and your calling?

Discovery Method 4: Holy Anger

What makes you angry? I'm not talking about traffic, or grapes with seeds in them. (I hate those!) I mean the thing in this world that just turns your stomach, that you cannot tolerate. That anger may be from God—and the key to discovering your calling.

Moses is a great example. At one point Moses saw an Egyptian mistreating an Israelite slave. Moses couldn't stand it, and in his anger he killed the Egyptian. So is it surprising that later his calling from God became freeing the Israelites from slavery in Egypt?

My wife cannot tolerate that there are more people in slavery today than at any point in the history of the world, and that most of these slaves are abducted young girls forced into prostitution. So she's back in school getting her master's degree in counseling in hopes that she can help girls who have been rescued out of sex slavery.

So what makes *you* angry? That some people can't find freedom from their addictions? The plight of the homeless? That there are people who are far from God and have been turned off by the church? That some children will grow up without fathers? Marriages ending in divorce? Pregnancies ending in abortion? Racism?

Perhaps that anger is from God, and he wants you to do something about it.

Discovery Method 5: Deep Gladness

You've identified what rouses your anger, now let's think about what makes you happy. Not happy like grapes without seeds in 'em (I love those!), or when Easter is getting close and Cadbury Eggs go on sale. I'm talking about what you do that makes you feel alive, that you'd just keep doing forever if you could.

Frederick Buechner writes that God calls us to do work (a) that we need to do and (b) that the world needs to have done. If you really get a kick out of your work, you've presumably met requirement (a), but if your work is writing cigarette ads, the chances are you've missed requirement (b). On the other hand, if your work is being a doctor in a leper colony, you have probably met requirement (b), but if you're bored and depressed by it, chances are you have not only bypassed (a) but probably aren't helping your patients much either. The place God calls you is the place where your deep gladness and the world's deep hunger meet.[1]

What makes you angry can expose one of the world's deep needs; what makes you *happy* can identify your *deep gladness*.

So what makes you happy? Teaching kids? Organizing? Sharing your faith with people who are far from God? Planning an event? Fixing cars? Writing? Making something good even better? Photography? Leading a team? Meeting new people?

Your answer may be one of the puzzle pieces that come together to reveal your calling.

Discovery Method 6: Clearness Committee

Parker Palmer has a great little book about discovering your calling titled *Let Your Life Speak*. Palmer tells the story of a time when he was offered a job he planned on taking. But he comes from a Quaker background. The Quakers have a tradition called a "Clearness Committee."* When a person is faced with a decision having to do with their calling, they meet with a few

*Don't be jealous just because the Quakers have all the cool stuff.

wise friends. These friends ask a series of questions designed
to help discern whether this new job is truly a part of God's
calling on that person's life.

I don't know much about Quakers beyond their skills with
oatmeal, but I like this idea. The Bible teaches that we are experts
at self-deception and that there is wisdom in many counselors.
So if you're trying to discover your calling, one way to do it is
to ask others. Email a bunch of friends and ask them what they
think, or bring together a small group of wise people who know
you well, hand out some rice cakes, and ask them to ask you a
bunch of questions.

Discovery Method 7: Strengths

What are you good at? God gave you gifts and abilities, and they
serve as clues as to what God wants you to do with your life.
The Bible compares us to body parts,[2] and I think a lot of us
are thumbs trying to be elbows, and intestines serving as noses,
and ears attempting to be feet. God made you uniquely you for
a unique reason. Function follows form. In architecture, it's the
opposite—what you're going to do in a building determines
how you should build it, so form follows function. But not so
with you. With you, what God made you determines what you
should do. So you can understand your function only after you've
discovered your form.

So what are you good at? I've met a lot of people who get
delusional when it comes to this question. Some think they're
not good at anything. That's wrong. God didn't make you without gifts and abilities. Others think they're good at something
when they're actually awful. (Just watch the first few weeks of
American Idol.)

To determine what you're actually good at, you may want to
take some "tests." There are tests (both spiritual and secular[3])
that will help you discover your areas of strength.

This also could be a function your Clearness Committee plays
in your life. Get some *honest* people and ask them what they see

as your strengths. If necessary, give them a huge list of options. Explain to them that you need the truth. Don't ask them what they see as your weaknesses—your skin may not be thick enough to take it. Just ask for strengths and accept what they tell you.

Discovery Method 8: Low-Cost Probes

How do you discover your calling? We've looked at a bunch of "heady" techniques, but here's a more hands-on one: experiment. Bob Buford, author of the book *Halftime*, suggests doing "low-cost probes." Basically, find ways to try a new calling on for size without giving up your day job.

Perhaps you're feeling called to ministry? Ask your pastor if you can shadow him for a few days. Does it seem like something you could do? Thinking about going to film school? Tell your church you'd like to film and edit a few videos for them. Praying about becoming foster parents? Volunteer with the local Big Brother or Big Sister program to see how you do with a kid who starts out a needy stranger. Perhaps you're feeling called to become a teacher? Well, volunteer to teach in the children's ministry and see if it feels right. Considering becoming a missionary in Mexico? Get your lunch at Taco Bell tomorrow.*

If you have an idea about what your calling might be, what low-cost probes would allow you to kick the tires before you buy the car?

How Is God Calling You?

God is calling you. He's calling you not only to intimacy with him but also to influence in the world. He's calling you out of your comfort zone and to a compassionate life of serving. But *how* is he calling you? And to what is he calling you? That is the question, and it's time for you to answer it.

*Three of these four suggestions are great, one not so much. I'll let you figure out which is which. (I can't do all the work for you!)

Your Renegade Assignment . . .
Should You Choose to Accept It

Admit it: for years you've been dreaming about being a Quaker. Well, praise that guy on your oatmeal box, this is your chance! You're going to form a Clearness Committee and they're going to help you discern your calling.

Who to ask? People who know you well, love God, and have wisdom.

What to tell them? You want to discern your calling, and you need their help. Their role won't be to give you advice or to psychoanalyze you, but instead to ask you open-ended questions and trust that as you answer them God will work in you and move you toward discerning your calling.

What should they ask? Well, hopefully, God will lead them and they won't need your direction. And once they begin and you give some answers, there will be follow-up questions and things will flow. But in case they need some guidance to get started, here are some ideas:

- What do you do that makes you feel alive?
- If you had to attend a twelve-hour lecture on a topic, what would it be?
- What is one of the accomplishments of which you're most proud?
- For what skill or gift do others often compliment you?
- If you won the lottery and could volunteer full-time, what would you want to do?
- If you had the power to solve one world problem, which one would it be?
- What do you do that, while you're doing it, makes time fly by?
- Do you prefer to work on tasks or spend time with people?
- If you looked at your entire life as though it were a movie, what might the story line be?
- Where does God seem to "show up" most in your life?

So, what are you waiting for? Go. Do it. Now. Go to the Clearness Committee. Go directly to the Clearness Committee. Do not pass the Lewelling Quaker Museum. Do not collect 200 Quaker oatmeal cookies.

10

Caution Your Calling

I have ADD and DDD: Attention Deficit Disorder and Dare Devil Disorder. These two afflictions cause me to avoid caution signs—sometimes because I don't notice and sometimes because I just don't care.

One time I was skiing with some friends from high school and we came across a "Warning: This Slope Closed! Do Not Enter!" sign. My DDD kicked in and I said, "Guys, we've got to do this!" Soon we were shouting and skiing down the slope—and then we were screaming and stopping as we saw there was no more slope. Before us was a cliff with a twenty-foot drop. We could try to climb back up the mountain, or we could make a jump fit for the X Games. We made the jump, not with laughter and anticipation but with fear and trepidation.

Another time I drove my friends to a concert. After the concert we jumped in my car and sped away in an attempt to avoid the traffic jam we knew was coming. I took a quick right and was greeted by a thousand headlights pointed directly at me. My friends started yelling, "We're going the wrong way!" and "It's a one-way street!" and I was yelling, "Shut up! I already figured that out!" and "Tell me what to do about it!" and "We're going to die!" Unfortunately, my ADD had led me to miss the sign that would have allowed us to avert the crisis.

Or another time I was in Israel with some pastors exploring a biblical site. As we walked around we came across a path with a warning sign: "Do Not Enter." "The sign isn't very clear," I argued. "What are they trying to hide from us?" I questioned. "What could be down that path? The ark of the covenant? The shroud of Turin? Perhaps Jesus himself is down the path, and we're going to miss our opportunity to see him because of a stupid sign! I don't think so!" Soon three of us were walking down the path. The other two of "us" were judging the three of us for our social deviancy and lack of good judgment. What was down that path? We didn't find anything. But at one point a tour group looked over a ridge with great expectancy only to see . . . the three of us. Not wanting to disappoint them, we pretended we were the three members of the Trinity, but I think I was unconvincing in my portrayal of the Holy Spirit.*

Caution!

Discovering your calling can be an important part of starting to live a dangerous, faith-filled life for God. There's often great relief and joy when we discern what God wants us to do for him in his world. But . . . there are also some dangers we need to be aware of when discovering our calling. And if we ignore the caution signs, we can end up in a place we really don't want to be.

Calling Caution 1: Difficult, Draining, Depressing

The Bible tells us that God's will for our lives is "good, pleasing, and perfect."[1] And that's true, but we don't want to romanticize. This doesn't necessarily mean wealth, status, security, great benefits, and a lifetime supply of happiness and peanut butter cups. In fact, basically every person in the Bible who discovered

---

*Next time I'll do more than just make wind noises with my mouth.

their calling from God *didn't want it*. Read the stories, from Moses to Gideon to Jeremiah. They didn't want their calling but they said yes because it was from God, and they found out that God's will was good, pleasing, and perfect. But it was also difficult, draining, and sometimes depressing. Moses led a huge group of whiners. Gideon risked his life in battle. Jeremiah shared God's message and *no one* responded. Good, pleasing, and perfect . . . AND difficult, draining, and depressing.

That may sound like a contradiction, but it's not. In fact, it's the story of *my* calling. What God has asked me to do is good, pleasing, and perfect—*and* difficult, draining, and depressing. And I wouldn't choose anything else because there is great reward and comfort in knowing I'm doing what God made me to do.

Calling Caution 2: The Waiting Is the Hardest Part

God's calling on your life typically includes a promise, such as: *You're going to start a church that will reach people far from God*. Or: *You're going to impact kids' lives*. Or: *Your kids will grow up to radically love God and love people*. Or: *You'll help alleviate poverty and hunger in your city*.

For instance, when God called Abraham to leave his home, he promised to bless him and give him descendants who would be God's people.

That's cool. Who doesn't want a promise from God? But here's the caution: we often have to *wait* to experience the promise. And it might be a long wait. God promised Abraham descendants, and I'm sure Abe and his wife got busy, then ran to the store to get the home pregnancy test. But it was negative. And Mrs. Abe didn't get pregnant the next day either, or the next week, or month, or year. It was *decades* later when God delivered on his promise. Why the wait? I don't know, but God does.

You may have to wait for years before getting going on your calling, or you may start immediately but toil in obscurity without seeing results for decades. You may even forget the promise.

But God won't. So answer the call, stay faithful, and wait patiently but expectantly.

Calling Caution 3: Incomplete Picture

When we start to discover our calling, part of the problem is that typically we only *start* to discover our calling. What I mean is that God doesn't give us a complete picture. God called Abraham to leave his home and go, but didn't tell him where he was going! How do you use GPS to route that one?

In the same way, God may tell you how to get moving toward your calling without showing you where the trip is going to take you. Why? Perhaps because not knowing where you're going makes it feel like a dangerous journey. It requires faith and forces us to stay dependent on God.

Calling Caution 4: The Fear Factor

Perhaps the best thing about discovering your calling is that it induces near-vomiting levels of fear. (Sorry, my native language is sarcasm.) When I realized back at seminary that God was calling me to start a church from scratch, I could almost feel the pee trickling down my leg. My wife is now planning on ministering to young girls who have been abducted, brainwashed, and forced into drug addiction and prostitution. Trust me, she's nervous. When God serves you your calling, it will taste like fear.

Why is there fear?

Well, God typically gets us moving in the right direction *without* showing us the destination. That induces fear. God generally calls us to things that seem bigger than us, perhaps even impossible. He does that because it then takes faith on our part.

What God calls us to do may not be normal. It may not be what others expect of us. It may not be what we've always done. That can be a bit embarrassing or intimidating or scary.

If you're not willing to stare down fear, you're probably wasting your time trying to discover your calling. And if you get a calling that doesn't induce fear, you should at least consider the possibility that it may not actually be your calling.

Calling Caution 5: Free Falling

Once you've discovered your calling and move toward it, you'll expect wind rushing through your hair; you'll be saying great quotes about how you were made for a moment such as this and are feeling God's pleasure, and you'll see amazing results. Perhaps you'll even be asked for your autograph. And all of that may happen. But here's something even more likely: you will fall down. You will start moving, and then fall. And fall again. You'll be confused. *I thought God called me to do this? Maybe this isn't my calling? I thought I was made to do this? Why am I not good at it? Why is it so unnatural for me?*

The answer? Because it's *new* for you. When you volunteer for the first time in the children's ministry, or share your faith for the first time, or give your first sermon, or film and edit your first video, it's just not going to go so great. There's a great theological term that explains this: normal. It's *normal* to not be great at something when you first start, even if you were made for it. Michael Jordan had some amazing innate abilities for putting a ball through a hoop, but I bet he missed his first few shots in his youth basketball league.

Don't let falling down or failing create doubt, and don't quit. No one starts out amazing. We all start out awkward. We gradually get more comfortable, we improve, wind starts rushing through our hair, women (or men) begin to swoon over us, and so forth. But on the way to "I was made for this," you will fall down. Perfectly normal.

Calling Caution 6: Not Dramatic

As you've read the last few chapters, maybe you've started dreaming about the exciting calling God has for you. But what if God has what feels like a "boring" calling for you? What if God calls you to something not so dramatic but requiring great faithfulness? What if it doesn't seem important?

A preacher named Fred Craddock once said, "To give my life for Christ appears to be glorious. To pour myself out for others, to be a martyr for Christ, I'll do it! I'm ready, Lord. I'll go out in a blaze of glory." He's saying that we think giving ourselves to God is like taking a $1,000 bill and placing it all on the altar, saying, "Here's my life, Lord. I'm giving it all." But then Craddock says, "The reality for most of us is that God sends us to the bank and has us cash in that $1,000 bill for quarters. And we go through life putting out 25 cents here and 50 cents there. Usually, giving our life to Christ isn't all that glorious. It's done in all of those little acts of love, 25 cents at a time."

He's right, but $1,000 in quarters can do a lot of good.

For instance, this book has an editor. You know my name, but not his. But this book wouldn't be in your hands without him.

Billy Graham had a mother who prayed for him and nurtured his faith. We'll never know much about her, but Billy Graham wouldn't have happened without her.

Mother Teresa probably had a nun who served as her role model. Churches need janitors. There are Christian grocery clerks who are making a huge difference in the world through each caring interaction with customers. If someone wasn't in the church nursery holding the crying baby, mom and dad couldn't be in the sanctuary hearing the gospel for the first time. There are faithful garbagemen who show the love and joy of Christ through their hard work and the way they smile and wave all morning long.

Calling Caution 7: Target

Here's the last caution I'll mention, and it's the one you don't want to hear. If you discover your calling and start living in it, you'll become a target of Satan. It may sound like a Church Lady kind of thing to say, but it's true.

The Bible warns us that the devil prowls around like a lion looking for someone to devour.[2] And if you actually start making a difference for God, the target on your back lights up like neon. The hippie dude in my preaching class was right: when we start to make a difference for God, the devil is going to jump us.

But there's good news. The Bible encourages us that "the eyes of the LORD range throughout the earth to strengthen those whose hearts are fully committed to him."[3]

The Bible also warns us that Satan is a thief who wants to steal, kill, and destroy your spiritual life and the impact you can have in this world.[4] If you begin to follow your calling, you may appear on Most Wanted signs in hell.

But the Bible also encourages us that our ally Jesus is in us, and he is greater and more powerful than the enemy of our souls.[5] Jesus will give us a life full of God and making a difference for him.[6]

So will discovering your calling make you a target? Yes.

Can you keep the devil off your back? No.

But can God do that for you? Yes.

Is the impact you make in the world for God worth the target on your back?

Absolutely.

11

Avoid Your Other Calling

One of my favorite authors writes about a men's retreat he attended where the guys sat in a circle and discussed their calling. They were each encouraged to talk about the mission God had for their lives, and they were challenged to think about how they might miss it and instead live out a "shadow mission."

Just as we all have a mission—a way of contributing to God's kingdom that we were designed and gifted for—we also have what might be called a shadow mission. My shadow mission is what I will do with my life if I drift on autopilot. It consists of the activities toward which I will gravitate if I allow my natural temptations and selfishness to take over. Everybody has a shadow mission.

By way of illustration, one of the staff members told us, "My shadow mission is to watch television and masturbate while the world goes to hell." A round of nervous laughter swept across the circle of men.

"I'm going to say it one more time," the man said, "only this time I want you to listen and not laugh." And then he said it again: "My shadow mission is to watch television and . . ."

This time the silence was sobering. Each of us was thinking the same thing: how easily any of our lives can slide into such a self-centered, trivial pursuit. He wasn't tempted to be Adolph Hitler or Saddam Hussein. The man would have fought against that kind of outright evil. It was the banality of his shadow mission that made it so possible.[1]

God has a calling for each of our lives, but there's a problem. God typically calls us to an uncomfortable mission. We prefer our calling to be *comfortable*, thank you very much.

And so we refuse to give ourselves to God's mission for our lives. But we *will* give ourselves to something. Something will become the object of our obsession. Something will be what we pour our time into. Something will be our attempt at greatness.

And our "somethings" tend to be things that are safe and selfish.

Love God, Love People, and . . .

The way we express our mission at my church is:

Love God, Love People, Turn the World Upside Down

We're to have intimacy with God and people, and then have influence on the world according to the unique way God made us. But I could express *my* personal mission this way:

Love God, Love People, Win Fantasy Football

If I'm honest, I generally prefer to pour myself into making sure my fake football team wins in my fake football league instead of having a real, eternal impact with my life. A guy I spend time with every week would probably say his personal mission is:

Love God, Love People, Play Video Games

It's true. His every spare moment is devoted to playing Xbox. His biggest goals in life are defeating people he's never met who play against him online. I have a bunch of friends who could express their mission this way:

Love God, Love People, Make Sure My Kids Grow Up to Become Successful

Sure, we could argue that if their kids end up successful, the parents maybe had some influence on the world through them. But that's *not* their motivation. They want their kids to have what they never had, or they are driven by fears about their kids' futures. They may have a need to prove themselves through their kids, or they've totally embraced the American Dream even though it doesn't match God's dreams.

And we all know guys whose mission is:

Love God, Love People, Root for My Team! (Because We Rule!)

I'm a big sports fan, but this has always struck me as funny. We use "we" when referring to our sports teams, but our sports teams don't know we exist. If we suddenly changed our allegiance (which we would never do) and started rooting for another team, the rest of "we" wouldn't know, or care. The Los Angeles Dodgers would not start texting each other, "Vince Antonucci just defected to the Tampa Bay Rays! What do we do? How will we continue without him?" Nor would the Rays celebrate my arrival. "There's a new member! This is the day when everything changes for us! World Series, here we come!" Our sports teams don't know we exist, but we live and die with their wins and losses.

And I know other people who could express their mission one of these ways:

Love God, Love People, Sculpt My Body at the Gym
Love God, Love People, Get My Political Party Elected
Love God, Love People, Watch Television Six Hours a Day
Love God, Love People, Fall in Love!

Why?

Embrace the Fear

Why do I prefer to hide in my office at church after the service, checking my fantasy football score, rather than being in the lobby with hurting people who need me? Why do we sit on our couches and watch other people live their lives on our flat screen, when there's a life out there for us to live? Why are we more passionate about our team winning the game than about the eternal impact we can make with our lives?

Deep down, I think we're afraid.

If I walk out in the lobby, well, someone might express their hurts to me, and I might not know what to say.

If I get off my butt, leave my living room, and start volunteering, well, what if it ends up being too much for me and is just draining?

If I start focusing on making an eternal impact with my life, well, what if I don't?

It's so easy to let fear lead us to miss our mission and settle for a shadow mission. We need to learn to embrace the fear.

In fact, if your calling isn't intimidating, it's likely not from God.

Embrace the fear. It means your life is going to be about something bigger than yourself.

Embrace the fear. You don't want to get to the end of your life and realize you never did anything you couldn't have done apart from the power of God.

Embrace the fear. You have a God who is bigger than what scares you, who is on your side, and who will walk with you as you venture out in faith.

Embrace the fear.

12

Set Yourself on Fire in the Darkness

received an email with an unexpected subject line: "Nudist Colony Gig Confirmed." The email was from the owner of the comedy show I was in. He wrote:

Team, Good News. Well, weird news, but good news! A nudist colony near San Bernadino recently voted to hire us to provide entertainment on Saturday, July 17th. . . . And no, they aren't expecting us to perform in the nude. However, they are fine with it so hey, "When in Rome!" Katherine (aka: Nipplerella) is going to most likely emcee the show and plans to perform in her whip cream bikini. Whoever goes will obviously have to be comfortable with a nude environment. You can either leave after the gig or choose to stay but if you stay there understand that all guests have to at least be partially nude to be out and about. (No pun intended.)

I had to laugh.

Experts encourage people who are nervous when speaking before an audience to picture everyone naked. But what if they *are* naked? Do you picture them with clothes *on*? Or is there some way of picturing them *more* naked?

I said no to the opportunity.

I guess I now need to explain how I even ended up in a stand-up comedy show.

Penetrating the Darkness

I had lived in Virginia Beach for twelve years before moving to Las Vegas to shine God's light into the darkness. Vegas is known for its bright neon, but behind the glow, it's actually one of the darkest places on the planet.

I wanted people to see God. I wanted to show God's love and offer healing and hope, especially to hurting people, and especially to hurting people who worked on or lived around the Strip. In Las Vegas, they call it "the industry." Nightclubs and restaurants feature "industry nights" where they focus on bringing in those who work in gaming and entertainment and clubbing jobs. Obviously, they do this to make money off of these people. But who was focused on *helping* people in these professions?

I wanted to.

But how?

I knew I would be starting a church, so I could just start it and invite the community to come to me, but that seemed kind of backward and probably ineffective. I realized that the best thing would be to somehow get involved in life on the Strip.

I considered getting a dealer's license (poker or blackjack, not heroin or crack), but with all it would take to get the church started, I didn't have time for a job like that.

I briefly looked into jobs with companies that catered banquets on the Strip. I realized that Chippendales might be hiring, but to apply I would need to lose sixty pounds, pick up some barbells, and buy a thong, none of which appealed to me.

And then it hit me . . . I'm hysterical.

Well, *I* think I'm hysterical.

From the time I was about seven years old I had been making up jokes and characters to perform for my friends and grandparents, and I had gotten laughs.

I searched for "Open Mic Comedy Nights, Las Vegas" and found several, so I decided to give it a try. At the very least, going up on a stage in the heart of Sin City would give me a small taste of what it's like to be an entertainer on the Strip, and hopefully it would allow me to build some relationships and learn more about the lives of the people I had moved here to help.

Standing Up

I decided to try out stand-up for the first time somewhere other than Vegas. I figured I would bomb and should do so where no one would know me or *ever* know me. I was going to Austin, Texas, to speak at a conference and found out about an open mic night at a pizza restaurant there.

The restaurant has since shut down and I can venture a guess why: people eating there smoked pot while they ate. I'm serious. I walked in that night and thought, *I think I smell pot.*

I wonder if someone is smoking pot?

Ohhh, that guy is smoking pot.

And that guy.

And that lady.

And that guy.

And this was an open restaurant, with people coming in and out to pick up pizzas and watch the comedy show.

I had heard Austin was weird, but this was really weird.

I signed up to perform, and the guy in charge told me they'd call me up soon. Finally it was my turn. I hit the stage, smiled, and said . . .

"Do you ever have a day where you don't have to work and . . ."

Some stoner interrupted me by calling out, "Dude, we don't have jobs."

"Yeah," another joined him, "jobs suck."

"Okay," I continued. "Well, if you don't have to work, you ever have a day where you can sit and watch television all day and . . ."

"That's all we do, dude. We watch television," the stoner guy informed me.

"Yeah, okay." I didn't want this to be a conversation with the guy, but it was quickly becoming one. "And you can sit and watch television all day and you end up watching a marathon of a show. Where they show like an entire season of a show in one day? Well, one time . . ."

"Awwww, dude, I know what you're talking about!"

It was a nightmare in a cloud of smoke. That guy will never remember it, but I'll never forget.

Going Pro

I went back to Vegas, not so sure whether or not I could cut it. I learned of a class for wannabe stand-up comedians. I signed up. I also went to one open mic night with somewhat better results than I had in the purple haze of the Austin pizza joint.

The first night of the class we each had to go up, say our name and how many times we had done stand-up, and then do five minutes of material. I walked up, checked to see if anyone was smoking weed, and said, "My name is Vince Antonucci, and I've done two open mic nights," then launched into my jokes. When I finished, the teacher, who was a professional comedian, said, "You shouldn't be doing open mic nights. You should be getting paid."

The class turned out to be pretty bizarre. It didn't help a lot, but it did force me to listen to some strangely bad comedy from people who never should have tried stand-up.

It also made me develop material on why I don't eat fish, extra virgin olive oil, Angel Soft toilet paper, and how there needs to be a *Yoda of Love* show on VH1.

I did make some friends, and it wasn't long before I was getting together with classmates to write new jokes. Soon the class was over, but I continued to do open mic nights most Sundays at a comedy club in a casino just off the Strip. Then I received an email. A local comedy show was having auditions. Would I please try out?

My first instinct was to say no. It seemed like too much of a time commitment. But then I noticed the details. The prelaunch core group for the church we were gearing up to start was meeting in the 305 Theater at the Greek Isles Hotel & Casino. The auditions were in the 305 Theater at the Greek Isles Hotel & Casino. Our meeting would end on Sunday by noon. The auditions were Sunday at 1:00. It was such an odd coincidence. I'd already be there. I would only need to hang out for an hour. I decided to do it.

When it was my turn, I went up onstage, did a few of my bits from the open mic nights, and then sat down to wait. When all the comics had auditioned, the judges left and we sat *American Idol* style, waiting to hear our fate. While everyone else was dying for a shot, I didn't really care. And whereas they had high hopes, I was sure I had no chance.

I was the first person called in to face the judges. I walked in and faced the panel, feeling more and more like an *American Idol* candidate. The lead guy said, "Congratulations, we want you to be in the show."

"Really?"

He nodded.

"How many people are you taking?" I asked, thinking that perhaps they were picking everyone.

"Three, and you're one of them."

And thus began my professional comedy career.

Toto, We're Not In . . .

My first night performing, I arrived early and walked into the dressing room to see a 350-pound man sitting in his underwear and putting on makeup. It was like, "Toto, we're not in Virginia Beach anymore. . . . WHAT AM I DOING HERE?!"

I soon learned that this man performed as a woman (named "Mona Lot") who stripped to end her (his?) routine.

The show also featured a woman named Nipplerella who performed in a bikini, and a man whose act consisted of him doing lewd things with balloon animals he made.

In fact, our show was so obscene that, after repeated warnings, the casino informed us they were kicking us out.

We were too obscene? For a casino? In Las Vegas?

The guy who ran the show started scrambling for a new venue and came up with the only all-nude strip club in Las Vegas. I dropped out.

At this point you may be wondering, "Why exactly were you in this comedy show?"

Light in the Darkness

One of my favorite things about Jesus is that he was very clear about who he was. He was the light of God, and he came to shine that light into the darkness. Jesus described himself by saying, "I am the light of the world. Whoever follows me will never walk in darkness, but will have the light of life,"[1] and "While I am in the world, I am the light of the world,"[2] and "The one who looks at me is seeing the one who sent me. I have come into the world as a light, so that no one who believes in me should stay in darkness."[3]

Jesus explained his ministry by quoting Isaiah 9:2, "The people walking in darkness have seen a great light; on those living in the land of deep darkness a light has dawned."

Somehow we've come to think of Jesus as hanging out in Christian coffee shops with the good people. But no, Jesus was the light of God. The purpose of light is to illuminate the darkness. When God sent Jesus, he sent him into the heart of darkness.

So Jesus went into Samaria, where no self-respecting Jew would go because the people there weren't God's people. In fact, Jews considered Samaritans worthless dogs. And Jesus befriended a woman who was living in the darkness of her sexual sin. Jesus was light to her, and it brought her new life.

Jesus went to Jerusalem where, instead of just visiting the synagogue, he went to a pool where the blind, lame, and paralyzed hung out. It was a place religious people would never go because the sick were considered cursed by God. Jesus befriended a guy and, for the first time, the light of God dawned in his life.

Jesus went to a party at a tax collector's house, a guy named Matthew. The religious leaders stood outside and judged Jesus for being there and associating with "those people." But they didn't understand that "those people" were the reason Jesus came. He came into the world, and into that home, as a light, so that "those people" would no longer have to stay in darkness.

Reading all those stories and thinking about Jesus's life here on earth, and how different it was from what he was used to in heaven, forces me to ask: How drastic must that difference have been? How big a shift was it to go from being in the presence of God to being in the presence of sinners? How vast was the difference from being worshiped by angelic beings to being worshiped by town prostitutes? To go from hearing angelic songs to hearing the coarse talk of salty fishermen?

Sent

So why was I in that comedy show? Because Jesus said, "As the Father has sent me, I am sending you."[4] Jesus was sent to be the light that shines in the darkness, and *we* are sent to be the light that shines in the darkness. Jesus said:

> You are the light of the world. A town built on a hill cannot be hidden. Neither do people light a lamp and put it under a bowl. Instead they put it on its stand, and it gives light to everyone in the house. In the same way, let your light shine

before others, that they may see your good deeds and glorify your Father in heaven.[5]

What's sad is that those verses perfectly describe most Christians—in reverse. It's as if Jesus said, "You are *not* the light of the world. A town on a hill that *can be* hidden. People light a lamp and put it under a bowl. That way it *doesn't* give light to anyone in the house. In the same way, *don't* let your light shine before men, otherwise they may see your good deeds and praise your Father in heaven," and Christians are obeying his words perfectly.

Most Christians are happy to grab some other Christians and put themselves under a bowl. Oh, they might put a Christian bumper sticker on the bowl, but Jesus said we'd be known by our love, not by the slogans we put on our cars. The Bible says that Jesus had life in him, and that life was the light that shone in the darkness.[6] It's our lives that let people see God, not our T-shirts. The problem is that too often we refuse to bring the light into the darkness.

That is a problem, because people need to see the light. If you're not close to people who are far from God, you're not as close to God as you think you are, because God's heart is always with those who are far from him. That's why he sent Jesus. It's why he sent me to Las Vegas and to a comedy show. And it's why he's sending *you*.

If you're not shining light into the darkness, you're shining for nothing. But the reality is that most Christians refuse to go into the darkness, and say no to the journey Jesus wants to send them on.

There are all kinds of reasons we say no. We begin thinking about building relationships with people who are far from God, and sharing our faith with those people, and leading them to Jesus—and the reasons we can't do it start to fly. "I can't do that because my life isn't a good enough example; I guess I'm not 'light' enough." "I can't share Jesus because I'm not very good at that." "I can't talk about my faith because I wouldn't know what to say." "I can't tell people about Jesus because I wouldn't know the answers to people's questions."

None of those excuses are legitimate because they're all about *you*. You're not the one who leads a person to Jesus. *God is*.

Really, when you boil down all those excuses, they reduce to fear. It just feels too dangerous, and we really prefer to play it safe. We prefer to play it safe even when people's lives and eternities are at stake.

But remember, we can trust the catcher. God's eye is on us, and his hand is ready to catch us should we start to fall. And don't forget: you can stare down the risk by staring at the potential return—there are people who are a mess, who are struggling with addictions, who are living life and facing eternity without God. That's why Jesus commanded us to do whatever it takes to rescue them from the darkness.

There was a movie that came out several years ago called *Man on Fire*. Denzel Washington starred in the role of Creasy, an ex-military assassin in Mexico City working as a bodyguard for a blonde seven-year-old girl named Pita, played by Dakota Fanning. Pita is kidnapped and then apparently executed by her kidnappers. Creasy, who had become very attached to Pita, is devastated and vows to do whatever it takes to get vengeance. He immediately plunges his life into the darkness of the child abductors' world in Mexico.

The leader of the gang that kidnapped Pita is known as "The Voice." After killing several of the people involved in the kidnapping, Creasy finds the brother and pregnant wife of "The Voice." He calls the Voice on the phone and demands a meeting. The Voice asks him, "How much do you want?" at which point Creasy shoots off all the fingers of his brother's hand and says, "I'm going to take your family apart piece by piece. You understand me? Piece by piece. I don't want your money. You understand me?" The Voice says, "I will give you a life for a life. I will give you her life for your life."[7]

Suddenly Creasy realizes that Pita is still alive, that she still has the hope of life. Creasy agrees to the Voice's proposition and sets up a meeting where the kidnappers release Pita. Creasy gives her a hug and surrenders himself to the kidnappers. Soon he loses his life.

When we think about people who are still living in the darkness, a lot of us assume they no longer have the hope of life, that there's nothing we can do for them. But Jesus came on a search and rescue mission for people kidnapped by the darkness, flooding this world with light for them. He said that his mission is now our mission.

As the Father sent him to be light in the darkness, to rescue people who still have the hope of life, God has sent us. It's a big part of the renegade life.

Your Las Vegas?

So what is your Las Vegas? You don't have to move to Sin City, but what pockets of sin in your community could you invade with God's light? Maybe you could start a ministry to a strip club in your area, or you could start dropping off donuts each week at the local Planned Parenthood.

And what's your comedy show? Is there a group you can get involved in where most of the people wouldn't know Jesus? Perhaps you ride a motorcycle and could join a club. Maybe there's a softball team in a city league you could join, or you could start a dodgeball team with people from work. Is there a person at your job whom everyone avoids but you could embrace? Maybe there's a kid you know whose home life is obviously a mess, and you could use your life to let him know he's loved.

We can't just hang out in Christian coffee shops with the good people. We must go straight into the heart of darkness. We have to, because we are God's light, and we can only serve our purpose if we're lighting the darkness. If we're going to be people who follow Jesus, we probably need to go pretty far and get quite uncomfortable. In fact, if we never ask, "What am I doing here?" maybe we're not truly following Jesus.

GOING ROGUE:

Your Renegade Assignment . . .
Should You Choose to Accept It

The last chapter ended with:

> We can't just hang out in Christian coffee shops with the good people. We must go straight into the heart of darkness. We have to, because we are God's light, and we can only serve our purpose if we're lighting the darkness. If we're going to be people who follow Jesus, we probably need to go pretty far and get quite uncomfortable. In fact, if we never ask, "What am I doing here?" maybe we're not truly following Jesus.

If you read this book and nod your head in agreement, but your life doesn't change, all you've done is deceive yourself. Renegades take action, and we're becoming renegades.

So . . . what's your Las Vegas? What dark place do you feel called to? If you haven't felt a direct call from God, settle for a holy anger or a disturbing restlessness. What is it?

- The school in your town where all the kids are on free or reduced lunches and live in homes surrounded by violence?
- The local sex store?
- The abortion clinic?
- The ostracized minority people group in your city?
- The loud kids with the drooping pants at the skate park?
- The street where the prostitutes hang out at night?

What's your Las Vegas? Got it? So now—you're going to go to them. Not to let them know they're wrong but to let them know they're loved. As you'll learn in the next chapter, it's love that turns a life around. And so you're going to love them in the most powerful but least weird way you can come up with. What will that be? You've got to figure that out, so start brainstorming and praying and talking to your friends.

When are you going to do this? Within four weeks. If you feel like you need some time to come up with an idea, or the resources it will require, or the guts you'll need, then put a date on your calendar (right now) for four weeks, or four weekends, from now. But if you can, do it sooner.

And when you do it, let me know how it goes: vince@renegadebook.com.

13

Lead with Love

The fact that there are people who are like sheep without a shepherd makes Jesus sick. It makes renegades sick as well. Jesus left heaven and went into the darkness to seek and save God's lost children. Renegades leave their comfort zones to be God's light in dark places, in hopes of returning God's kids to his arms.

That sounds right. We all probably agree with it.

But the truth is that it rarely happens. Most Christians aren't engaging those outside the faith. In fact, it's incredibly rare for a Christian to actually help someone far from God get close to God.

So how do we do it?

How do we do it in a way that's effective? How do we do it in a way that doesn't freak out people who are far from God?

There's a secret.

A Motorcycle Gang and a Tattoo Shop?

About a dozen friends joined us in moving across the country to start a new church in Las Vegas. One of those friends is Tommy.

Tommy was special ops for the Air Force and served in Iraq twice. He would get dropped from an airplane into enemy territory where he would do reconnaissance work.

When Tommy left the Air Force, he went to seminary and helped a new church get started. Later he came to my church in Virginia Beach, and then his family decided to help us launch a church in the middle of Sin City.

Tommy rides a motorcycle, so he joined a motorcycle club in Vegas. He figured he needed to make friends, especially friends who don't have Jesus, and so why not? Tommy started hanging out with these guys, looking for ways to serve them, helping out with events they planned. After some time, Tommy looked for opportunities to mention his faith and to invite them to church. These were *not* churchgoing guys, but they were open to Tommy's words. A few started coming. One brought his Wiccan girlfriend, one started volunteering, and one eventually gave his life to Christ.

Tommy is also into tattoos. After about a year in Vegas, he felt like God was sending him to the tattoo community. So Tommy got a job in a tattoo shop.[1] One of the tattoo artists was a girl named Heather. Tommy befriended her, listened to her problems, and helped her as he could, and pretty soon Heather started showing up at our church.

Another tattoo artist was Dylan. Dylan had never been to church and never read the Bible. When Dylan learned that Tommy was a Christian, he said he'd always had questions he'd like to ask one of "them." Dylan asked, "I've heard of Jesus, and I've heard of Mary. Do they have any connection?" "Yeah," Tommy told him, "Mary is Jesus's mother." "Oh." Dylan seemed surprised, and then asked, "So where does Mother Teresa fit in? Where's she at in the Bible?"

One day Dylan mentioned that he loved Harry Potter. Tommy told him he had never read or seen any of the Harry Potter series. Dylan was shocked. Tommy asked Dylan if he would watch the entire series of movies with him. Tommy had no interest in the movies, but he knew it was a chance to build their relationship.

They watched hours and hours of Harry Potter together, and through it had some more conversations about Christianity. And then Dylan started coming to our church. A couple of months ago Dylan told Tommy that he wanted to follow Jesus, and Tommy baptized him into Christ.

Davidson was another tattoo artist, but unlike Heather and Dylan, he wasn't just ignorant and oblivious about Christianity, he was adamantly opposed to it. He let Tommy know that he didn't believe in God, but if somehow there was a God, he hated him, hated Christians, and hated church. Davidson knew that some of the people from his shop were now attending Tommy's church but said he would never come. Tommy built a friendship with him and looked for opportunities to serve him. He heard that Davidson was moving, so he asked what time he should show up to help. The day after Thanksgiving he heard that Davidson loved Thanksgiving leftovers but had none as he had spent Thanksgiving alone. The next day Tommy brought him all the leftovers from his meal. Guess what happened? Davidson started asking Tommy, "So what's all the hype about your church?" Last Sunday Davidson showed up for the first time.

Truth and Love

We all need truth and we all need love, and what Christians have to share with people is truth and love.

The fear a lot of us have about sharing Jesus, and what keeps us from doing it, is that we think of it as trying to convince people of our truth. We're not effective because most people don't want to be convinced of anything. Not many people are walking around thinking, *I hope someone convinces me that I'm wrong about some big stuff today.*

But people *do* want to be loved. They may not walk around consciously thinking about it, but they do want to be loved. We're not afraid of loving people. We are afraid of trying to convince people they're wrong and that we have this exclusive truth they need to believe, but we're not afraid to love people.

The problem is that we focus on truth and lead with truth when we need to focus on love and lead with love. That's what Jesus did. He came to give us truth and love,[2] but he focused on and led with love.

Maybe the most remarkable thing about Jesus's life is that he was the one sinless person to ever walk the face of the planet, and yet everywhere he went the most sinful people were drawn to him like a magnet. Typically "more sinful" people avoid "more sinless" people—it just makes you feel worse about yourself to be around someone who is obviously better than you. But that wasn't the case with Jesus. Jesus went to parties where sinners gathered around him. He spent time with all sorts of disreputable men and women. We see prostitutes pouring perfume on his feet. Tax collectors chose to hang out with him.

Why? Why did sinful people want to be around Jesus? I think it's because Jesus didn't make them feel worse. He made them feel *loved*. Jesus knew a secret that Christians today have lost: it's love that turns a life around. The way to change a life is not by judging people for their wrongdoing but by embracing them in spite of it; not by pointing out their sins but by pointing the way to hope.

If we're going to follow Jesus into the darkness and help people there to find him, we also need to follow his methodology. We need to lead with love. We have to speak the truth, but we must lead with love.

We see Jesus do this time and time again, like when he came into the town of Jericho, where the most hated man was Zacchaeus. Zacchaeus was hated—not just because as a tax collector he had extorted some extra money from the locals but because he was a Jewish man who had sided with the Romans. Back then Roman soldiers were coming into towns, putting up statues of Caesar, and commanding the people to bow down and worship. Anyone who refused would be massacred. There are accounts of thirty to forty thousand men, women, and children being impaled at one time on poles outside their hometown. Once they had established their authority, the Romans would tax the people. An astronomical amount of money was required to fund Rome's massive army. Historians estimate that the average Jewish household could pay 90 percent of their income in taxes to Rome. Zacchaeus was collecting taxes from the Jews to pay for the Roman army who had annihilated so many of the Jewish people.

So when Jesus came into town, did he condemn Zacchaeus? Did he make him feel worse? If anyone deserved it, he did. Jesus certainly would have been justified in leading with truth: "Zacchaeus, how dare you? You've betrayed God and God's people. You need to repent." But that's not what he did. Jesus led by saying to Zacchaeus, "I must stay at your house today."[3] Jesus led with love. He invited himself over to Zacchaeus's house to begin building a relationship. And what ended up happening? "But Zacchaeus stood up and said to the Lord, 'Look, Lord! Here and now I give half of my possessions to the poor, and if I have cheated anybody out of anything, I will pay back four times the amount.'"[4] Zacchaeus's life was changed.

People need truth, and people need love, but it's critical that we follow Jesus's example and *lead* with love. Because it's love that builds a relationship, love that opens a person's ears to hear what you have to say, love that opens their heart to the Good News, and love that leads them to life change.

That's why Jesus led with love. Reading through the story of his life, you don't see him condemning people—except for the Pharisees, who were prideful and judgmental religious leaders who had no love and no use for it. But when Jesus met a person caught in sin, he led with love and then he gracefully spoke truth, and it turned people's lives around.

A few years ago I co-led a session at a conference with a pastor named Cal Jernigan. Our topic was "Preaching to the Unconvinced." Cal talked about how people who don't have Jesus need to know you like them before they'll listen to what you have to say. He explained that in most churches you're asked to behave ("If you're going to hang out with us we expect you to behave; no more sinning!"), then you're asked to believe, and once you do all that, finally you can belong. He explained how his church had reversed the order. Immediately you'll be accepted and befriended. Then the hope is that you'll grow to believe. And it's only after you believe that there's any assumption you'll start behaving.

Then I spoke about being grace wholesalers, as Jesus was, and about leading with love, as Jesus did.

During the question and answer time, Cal was at the mic and I was sitting. Cal fielded a few easy questions, and then a big guy in the back raised his hand. His face was flushed beneath his trucker hat, and he yelled, "You know what? I hear you two talking about how you like sinners! And you love sinners! But what I want to know is: When do you call sin *sin*? When do you tell sinners that they're sinners? When do you preach about sin and hell?"

Cal said, "That is a great question, and Vince has a great answer for you." Then he walked away.

Thanks, Cal.

So I stood up, took the mic, and said, "Sir, I appreciate your question, but I would encourage you, instead of assuming, to go to our website and listen to our sermons, and you tell me if I preach about sin and hell. In fact, all you have to do is listen to our sermon from this past Sunday, and you tell me if I preach about sin and hell.

"But let me ask *you* a question: When you read the Gospels, where do you see Jesus going up and calling sinners *sinners*? Or do you see Jesus leading with love, establishing a relationship, showing a person he cared, and then helping that person to see where they need to change? And don't we want to follow the example of Jesus?

"You made an assumption about me; let me make one about you: I'm sure you talk to people about their sin, and I *know* I talk to people about their sin. The only difference is that when I talk to them about it, *they listen to me*. And I bet people *don't* listen to you. And the reason they listen to me is because I lead with love. I establish a relationship first."

Then I asked, "Will someone walk me to my car? 'Cause I'm afraid Trucker Hat Guy is going to beat the crap out of me!"

Easier to Judge

For some reason I don't understand, it seems much easier for most Christians to judge than to love. In fact, many Christians seem to think it's our responsibility to judge, and we shouldn't show love to someone until they start behaving—but that's the opposite of what Jesus did. Honestly, it's absurd.

Why?

Shawn Hornbeck disappeared on October 6, 2002, when he was eleven years old. After his disappearance, his parents quit their jobs, depleted their savings, and borrowed heavily as they devoted their lives to searching for him. But after four years they had given up hope. Then the phone rang one day. The voice on the other end was that of a local prosecutor. He said, "We think we've found Shawn. We're 95 percent sure."

Shawn's father says, "Those were the sweetest words that we have heard in our lives." Soon Shawn, now fifteen years old, was reunited with his parents.

Now let's imagine that phone call going a bit differently. Let's pretend the prosecutor said, "We think we've found Shawn. We're 95 percent sure. There's only one problem. It turns out that while Shawn was living with his kidnapper he developed the habit of shoplifting."

How do you think Shawn's parents would have responded? Do you think they'd say, "Well then, we don't want him back"? Or perhaps, "Well, please tell Shawn that he can come back home, but only after he cleans up his act. There will be no shoplifters in our home!"

No way.

I'm sure they would have said, "Shoplifting? Who cares if he was shoplifting? Just bring him home. We need to hold him! We'll talk to him about shoplifting later. In fact, we're confident that once he's back home and experiences our love and provision, he won't feel the need to shoplift anymore. But we're not worried about that right now. We just want him home!"

So why is it okay for us not to judge sin and to instead lead with love?

That's why.

I understand the fear people like Trucker Hat Guy have. The fear is that people will mistake grace for an acceptance of sin, maybe even take it as a license to sin.

If they mistake grace for an acceptance of sin, it is a mistake on their part, because they're not the same. An attitude of accepting sin says, "God loves you just the way you are, so keep doing whatever you're doing." The attitude of grace says, "God loves you just the way you are, but he loves you way too much to leave you that way."

An attitude of accepting sin says, "Come as you are, and don't feel any need to change." The attitude of grace says, "Come as you are, but don't stay that way."[5]

They are different, but the reality is that some *will* mistake grace for an acceptance of sin. And regardless of what Trucker Hat Guy tells you, it's worth the risk. How do I know that? Because God is willing to take that risk, and therefore so should we. God's grace is so amazing and outlandish that people *do* mistake it for an acceptance of sin. That's the way it's *always* been. Check out Romans 6 and you'll see that it was happening two thousand years ago.

And so if God is willing to offer a grace so amazing, knowing that some would mistake it for acceptance of or a license to sin, shouldn't we also be willing to take that risk?

We hope people won't make that mistake, but we offer grace regardless. We speak the truth but lead with love.

The Good News

The good news is that this makes helping people who are far from God get close to God a very real possibility for you.

114

People want to be loved, and you can love them. And as you love them you will be opening them up to truth. Because you led with love, it will be easier to share truth than you'd ever imagine.

Case in point: we have a lady who started coming to our church whom I'll call Kerry. It was obvious to me that Kerry was a lesbian, but I didn't mention it. I just loved her. I built a friendship with her week by week in the lobby of our church and in a class I taught that she attended. Little by little I earned her trust as she understood who I was and that I cared about her. Finally, after months of attending, Kerry approached me, "All right, I have to ask," she said. "Does the Bible really say homosexuality is wrong?"

I gave her a sympathetic smile and said, "Sorry, but yeah, it does."

Kerry looked into my eyes and said, "Do you know what I love about you? You've never once told me what I want to hear."

Why did she feel that way? Why was she able to hear and accept what was for her an extremely hard truth? Because I led with love. It's love that builds a relationship, love that opens a person's ears to hear what you have to say, love that opens hearts to the message, and love that leads to life change.

In fact, it was only a short time later that Kerry came over to my house, accepted Jesus as the lover and leader of her life, and got baptized in my swimming pool.

14

Renegade Profiles

Travis

The first person we reached through our church in Las Vegas was a pimp named Travis. Well, technically, I guess he was an amateur pimp. But you know what momma always said: a pimp is a pimp is a pimp.

Travis grew up in the New York City area. Most people have blood running through their veins; Travis had *hustler*. He was a smooth-talking professional moneymaker. He sold anything he could sell: mix tapes, T-shirts, photographs, music. He repeatedly asked his father, "Where can I make more money? Where's the money at?" And his father repeatedly told him, "The money is in Las Vegas."

So he finally put his stuff, his wife, and their two babies in a truck and went west to Sin City.

It was a perfect fit.

Travis started showing up at nightclubs and strip clubs and asking, "How about you make me your photographer?"

They'd laugh and say, "We don't need a photographer."

"Sure you do," Travis would tell them, and pretty soon he was their photographer.

Then Travis started going up to the strippers, asking them, "How about you make me your photographer?"

He'd get weird looks. "I don't need a photographer."

"Sure you do," he'd say, and soon Travis was photographing Vegas strippers.

Then Travis was sleeping with Vegas strippers. Then Travis's wife found out, and she moved out with the kids. But Travis was okay with that, because he had other girls now. He would tell them his story, and where he was going, then he'd ask, "You want to go where I'm going?" The girls would laugh and ask, "For real?" And Travis would smile and say, "Only one thing. If we're going to get where we're going, we're going to need some money. You know how to get some money?" And soon the girls were bringing Travis back the money they were making in the clubs and on the streets, excited to contribute to where they were going.

But somewhere deep inside, Travis knew that where they were going wasn't going to take him where he really wanted to be. Travis also wanted his wife back. He asked her to come back, but she refused. He asked how they could make their marriage work. She said she didn't know but, in desperation, wondered aloud if maybe the answer was God. Travis didn't think so, but he was willing to go to church on a Sunday morning if that's what she wanted.

That Sunday morning my message was "It Doesn't Matter." It doesn't matter who you are; God still loves you. It doesn't matter why you left; God is still pursuing you, just like the shepherd pursued the one lost sheep. It doesn't matter where you've been or what you've done; God will still take you back, just like the father took back the prodigal son.

After I spoke, this guy strode up to me. He looked cool and hip and kind of tough. He told me his name was Travis—and then he fell apart. He started crying uncontrollably. He was trying to talk, but I couldn't understand a word he was saying. I thought I made out, "I didn't know I was loved like that," but I wasn't sure. Finally, not sure what to do, I asked him, "Do you want to get together sometime?" He nodded, handed me a business card that identified him as "Doc Jones," and walked away.

A couple days later we met in a coffee shop. A couple months later we walked into a hot tub behind a pretty seedy casino hotel just off the Strip, and I baptized Travis. It was the first baptism in our new church. Travis's wife then walked down into the hot tub. She was our second baptism. Then, right by that hot tub, in front of the little group of people who made up our church, we did a rededication service for their marriage.

That day Travis *completely* gave his life to God. His heart was attacked by God's love, and now it bleeds gratitude. He experienced a grace explosion in the depths of his being, and he hasn't been the same since. He's become consumed. He'll do anything for God; he figures he owes him at least that.

Travis began asking us for invite cards. We make cards for people to give to their friends, and it's not uncommon for our people to take a couple. What is uncommon is for a person to take a couple hundred, but that's exactly what Travis did. He was giving them to everyone. He wanted them to know the God he now knew, to experience what he was experiencing. He decided a slight redesign of the cards would better reach his particular audience, so he got our permission then redesigned the cards and paid to have hundreds printed so he could use them.

Travis had a background in hip-hop music, so he started writing and recording songs about God and giving them out as free CDs. He learned that homeless people in Las Vegas desperately need socks, so he went to dozens of churches, asking if they'd help him collect new socks to give out. He then threw a block party in a poor urban area, giving countless pairs of socks to the homeless. Travis started thinking about the fact that college is when kids are making important decisions about their lives and it is also a tough time, especially if you go to college in the middle of Sin City. So he started hanging out at UNLV, made friends there, and was soon leading a Bible study full of students. And Travis thought about the people he had become friends with in his former life and started going back to visit them. Soon he was doing a one-on-one weekly Bible study with one of the major pimps in Las Vegas.

Travis is what a renegade looks like.

George

A few years after we started the church in Virginia Beach, I decided to pick about a dozen guys from the congregation I was impressed with and invite them into a group. We'd read a book a month, then get together to discuss it and how it applied to our lives.

Then I realized I would have to think through the hundreds of guys who attended our church and pick twelve. My first choice was easy: George. George was about fifty years old. He had served in the Navy years earlier but was now a car mechanic. George was full of joy, kind, generous, and encouraging. Honestly, with the other guys in the group, I hoped I could have an influence on them—but with George, well, I hoped he would have an influence on me. He was just an amazing guy.

I asked George to be in the group. He said yes. I told him he'd have to read a book a month. He said he didn't think he could. I rolled my eyes and asked him if we could meet to talk about it.

I ended up doing this book group for years, inviting different guys each year, and I had several tell me they couldn't read a book a month. The excuse was always the same: "I just don't have enough time." So we would meet, and I would ask, "So, what reality shows do you watch?"

And they'd say, "*Survivor* and *American Idol*."

And I'd ask, "So you have time to watch *American Idol*, but not to read a book that could help you grow and change your life?"

Or, "Do you watch sports?" I'd ask.

"Yeah, football on Saturdays and Sundays."

"So you have time to watch football, but not to read a book that could help you grow and change your life?" I'd keep meddling. "Do you play video games? Do you have time to surf the web?"

So, when George and I met for lunch, I explained, "George, if you're going to be in this group, I need you to read the book a month."

"I'll try." He didn't sound hopeful. "But I don't think I have the time to read it."

"Well," I suggested, "let's go through your schedule. What's your work schedule?"

George explained, "I work from eight to five, Monday through Friday. I get up at five a.m., so I can spend at least an hour praying and reading my Bible, then I make lunches for my wife and me to take to work, then we eat breakfast together before we leave, then I work till five."

"Okay." I was impressed. "Then what do you do?"

"I go home and make dinner for my wife, because she has to work till six. Then when she gets home, we eat."

"Okay, then what do you do at night?" This is where I was sure I had him. I was waiting to hear about Monday Night Football and reality television shows. But George explained how one night a week he went grocery shopping for his elderly mother, another night he led a Bible study, another night he met with a couple of guys he's trying to help grow, and another night he took his wife on a date.

At this point I was a bit desperate. "What about Saturday, George?" I asked.

Well, on Saturdays, it turned out, George fixed cars for free for people in need. On Sundays he went to church, then was a part of our homeless ministry. He was in charge of making sure there were clothes, blankets, and tents to give to the homeless.

By the end of the conversation I was defeated. "You don't have to read the book. You should write a book," I said.

I drove away from our meeting thinking, *The guy I want to become more like is the most servant-hearted person I've ever met. He pours his life out in serving others, and it gives him life.*

George is what a renegade looks like.

Monica

Monica grew up in Virginia Beach and has been a pediatric nurse for about twenty years. One day she was sitting in her church's service when her pastor (who many have described as ruggedly handsome, electrifyingly sexy, and amazingly brilliant—yes, me) talked about the village their church was adopting in Vietnam and how people would be able to serve that village with their American job skills. He mentioned how teachers might be able to train their teachers, computer programmers could help kids in the village learn to use a computer, nurses could provide medical care . . . and then he had Monica's attention. She knew she would be going to Vietnam. She had never done anything like that, never even considered anything like that, but now she knew she was going.

Monica went on her first trip five years ago. She's about to go on her sixth. That's six trips in five years. Each trip costs $2,400 and takes up all of Monica's annual two weeks of vacation.

On her first trip she had planned on providing medical care, but it turned out she helped to conduct a teachers' conference instead. Monica was disappointed that she couldn't use her skills but was still grateful for the chance to serve and build relationships. One day, when the mission team was about to leave the village, they heard yelling. A little girl was very sick and needed help. Monica took a deep breath and ran to get her medical supplies. The little girl had an abscess that had infected most of her upper leg. No one in the village knew what to do, but Monica did. She drained the abscess, applied antibiotics, and dressed the wound. The mother gave Monica a huge hug. Monica says she wasn't able to sleep that night because she couldn't stop praying for the girl. She later learned that the girl fully recovered and was back in good health.

Through her trips Monica has seen dramatic changes in the Vietnamese village. Atheistic, communist officials now thank Monica and her team for what they're doing for God. The people in the village who once viewed Monica with skepticism and as a tourist to whom they could sell things now greet her by name when she arrives, invite her into their homes, and share stories of how their families are doing. Several of the Vietnamese translators have come to faith in Christ.

God has used Monica in a powerful way, across the globe from where she lives, in a country where she can't speak the language, with a people group who couldn't be more foreign to her—and it's all because she was willing: willing to listen to God, willing to go, willing to sacrifice, and willing to be uncomfortable.

Monica is what a renegade looks like.

Matt

Matt grew up in the small, struggling manufacturing city of Richmond, Indiana. As a kid he went to church with his parents, but when he was eleven they started having marriage problems. They sought help from their church but were told they needed to "get right" with God before coming back to church. They never returned.

When Matt was thirteen his mother told him that she and his father were getting divorced. She said that his father had cheated on her. Matt hated his father for ruining his family. His father moved away, and Matt was now growing up fatherless.

Two years later Matt came home from school to find his mother asleep on her bed. Unable to wake her up, he called some of her friends and they discovered an empty pill bottle. She eventually woke up to learn that her attempt at suicide had been unsuccessful. The next morning Matt asked her why she had tried to kill herself. She told him, "I can't live any longer if you can't accept that I'm gay." Matt had no idea. He then realized that his father probably hadn't cheated on her. That wasn't the cause of their divorce.

Soon Matt's mother was living an openly gay life and would bribe fifteen-year-old Matt by purchasing alcohol for him so he would go out and get drunk so she could be alone with her girlfriends. Matt moved out when he was seventeen. By the time he was twenty-two he was divorced, had been homeless twice, and believed he was worthless.

A few years later Matt became friends with a youth pastor. The youth pastor invited Matt to hang out at his youth ministry meetings. Matt heard him tell kids week after week about God's love and how they could have a relationship with him. Finally Matt decided that was exactly what he wanted. He gave his life to Jesus and knew immediately that he wanted to go into ministry so he could help other people who were hurting and broken and without Jesus.

Matt graduated from Bible college and then served in several churches. Last year he was enjoying his job as the pastor of a church in Oklahoma when he visited his old hometown of Richmond, the town where he had experienced so much pain and had lived as a drunk on the streets. Driving around, he became overwhelmed by the idea that his old town was filled with people just like the old him. Something inside him snapped, and Matt and his wife and three kids moved from their comfortable life in Oklahoma to Richmond to start a church for people who are living the kind of life he used to live.

I get to coach Matt as a church planter, and every week I hear about how he is continually confronted with his past as he runs into people who knew him way back when. Sometimes he has to apologize for who he was and what he did. Sometimes he's shocked—as happened recently when he discovered that he had a nineteen-year-old son in Richmond he never knew about.

God is redeeming Matt's past, and in the same way that Matt was rescued, he's using Matt to rescue others.

Matt is what a renegade looks like.

Heidi

Heidi is from Savannah. Her husband is a pilot for FedEx. She used to have a daughter at home, but she's now grown and out of the house. Heidi came to our church on a mission trip.

We host lots of mission teams, and people always seem to be impressed with our ministry. And that was Heidi.

But there was something different about Heidi. She took what we're doing in Las Vegas and brought it back to Savannah. While in Vegas, she went to minister to the girls who work in strip clubs, and Heidi's heart broke for them. They were someone's daughters and they were God's children, but they were so far from him. So she decided to launch a strip club ministry in Savannah. A strip club ministry in Sin City is considered a little extreme, but in historic, Southern charm, mind-your-manners Savannah? It was beyond a stretch. But Heidi and a few other women from her church started praying and soon ventured into their first strip club.

It became immediately obvious that God was in this, because Heidi knew the owner. Heidi had chaperoned her daughter on a trip years earlier. The owner excitedly agreed to have Heidi and her team bring in a home-cooked meal for her girls every week. In fact, she was so appreciative that she offered Heidi a free lap dance the first time they brought in food. Heidi politely declined but passionately launched The Sunshine Girls ministry. They feed the employees of the strip club and show them God's love in a practical way, hoping to build friendships that might ultimately lead them to Jesus. They continue to go back every week, with the DJ announcing their arrival each time they come through the door. Girls have asked for Bibles, the owner has asked for prayer, and recently The Sunshine Girls have begun visits to two more strip clubs as they continue to bring the light of God into very dark places.

Heidi is what a renegade looks like.

Ethan, Matt, Doug, and Ryan

Ethan, Matt, Doug, and Ryan just graduated from college last year. They were friends at the University of Colorado. Every day I get to work with my friend Jake at my church, and he was the youth pastor for three of them back in Denver, when they were in high school. They struggled some in high school and partied some in college but realized that they were missing something, and that what they were missing was the most important something of all. They found their way back to God and together made a decision: they want to start a movement for Jesus.

The first step in their plan was a trip. Now guys who have just graduated college often take trips together—to the beaches of Cancun or backpacking through Europe, but this wasn't that kind of trip. This was a trip to seven countries that you wouldn't choose for a vacation. It was a trip to serve alongside missionaries in each location and to try to meet the needs of people who live there. They would be doing earthquake relief, providing clean water, fighting human trafficking, and delivering education. They saved their money and bought their tickets to each destination. The only thing they didn't purchase was a flight back home, because they're not sure when, or if, they'll return.

They're currently in Haiti, and the other day they wrote this on their trip blog:

> And now for a bit of real honesty. I've never been this uncomfortable in my entire life. I've felt emotions that I didn't even know I had and have been brought to my knees every day in a state of either confusion or fear. Every day is an unknown here. It's weird, it's the opposite of cozy, it gets intense, sometimes I wanna cry, and I love it. Because I've never felt this close to God in my entire life. I think when you follow God's calling to a place where you're in trouble if He doesn't come through, you'll be amazed at the big ways He shows up.[1]

Ethan, Matt, Doug, and Ryan are what renegades looks like.

You

You've just met a bunch of renegades. But what if those renegades met you? Would those renegades be meeting a fellow renegade? Is your story one that belongs in this book?

If not, here's what you need to know: every person in this chapter could point back to a time when he or she *wasn't* a renegade. For most of them, it wasn't even that long ago.

They weren't born renegades. They don't have a special gene that makes them superior to us. They weren't standing next to a nuclear reactor when it went off, radically altering their DNA. They're just normal people who at some point realized who God is and decided that they wanted to have intimacy with him and let it lead them to have influence in the world for him.

You can make that same decision.

You can decide that right now.

You can start your renegade story today.

GOING ROGUE:

Your Renegade Assignment...
Should You Choose to Accept It

What you're about to do is going to feel weird, but that's okay; renegades need to get used to feeling weird.

In the last chapter you read stories of some renegades. Your assignment is to write what your story might sound like if you truly became a renegade. I know, I know, you're not there yet. That's okay. At this point, this is just a vision, a dream, an act of faith. And it's just between you and God. So if you became a renegade and your life became what you'd want it to become, what would that look like?

_____

_____

_____

_____

_____

_____

_____

_____

_____

_____

_____

_____

_____

_____

_____

Answer this: the Bible says God can do more than we can dare to dream or imagine. So with God on your side, why can't this vision become your reality?

PART 4

REALITY FOR RENEGADES

Y ou want to be a renegade. You have an idea of what that life would look like. But there are some things you need to be aware of and be ready for before launching out into it.

As we conclude our journey together, I'm going to introduce you to a married couple who decided to be missionaries, a pastor who preached with machine guns pointed at him, a priest to lepers in Hawaii, and . . . the duck god. You'll also hear about my son's life-changing hamburger challenge experience.

And you will learn. You will learn what to do when God asks you to do something you don't want to do. You'll learn the magic ingredient that allows us to stay faithful to God when it seems impossible. You'll learn what to do while you're waiting. You'll learn what happens when you drift away from God and how to go back to him. You'll learn why people quit and how you cannot quit, so you can go out in a blaze of glory.

15

Hear What You Don't Want to Hear

In 1908 John Perkins and his wife found themselves aboard a steamship rounding the coast of Liberia. They were on this steamship because they were convinced God had called them to be missionaries in Africa. Unfortunately, God wasn't so specific as to tell them *where* in Africa, but they knew he wanted them in Africa.

As the steamship made its way around the northwest coast of Africa and through Garraway Bay, the Perkinses sensed God speaking to them again. He was telling them it was time to get off the ship.

They went to the captain, announcing that this was their destination and could he please bring them to shore? The captain refused, explaining, "I can't let you off the boat here. This is cannibal country. People go in there and never come back."

Everyone wants to hear from God—until he wants you to become someone else's lunch.

Do You Want to Hear from God?

Ask pastors what questions they receive most, and "How do I hear God's voice?" will be near the top of the list. It's a good question, because deriving direction from God, getting his guidance, receiving a word from the Lord is critical if we're going to do what he wants us to do.

But why is it so difficult?

Let me suggest that oftentimes we don't really *want* to hear from God. We think we do, but we don't. And one of the things that keeps us from living the renegade life is only listening when God tells us something we want to hear.

Think about this: Where in the Bible do we see someone who is glad to hear God's voice and get his direction? Where in the Bible is someone told something they want to hear?

Just about never.

God gave Adam and Eve only one simple command: "Don't eat the fruit of that tree over there." But it quickly became apparent that it was the one command they didn't want to obey.

Noah was asked to build a boat when it seemed no boat was needed, subjecting him to public embarrassment.

God asked Abraham to leave his home and go, but wouldn't tell him where.

God's plan for Joseph included an extended stay in prison. Sign me up!

Moses was asked to be God's stuttering spokesman and to defy the most powerful man in the world by leading the Israelite slaves out of Egypt.

Gideon received the assignment to lead a couple hundred men into battle against a couple thousand. Got to love those odds!

God told Isaiah to walk around through the towns completely naked for three years. I don't care how secure you are with your body; that's not something you volunteer for.

132

Ezekiel was told to lay on his side in the middle of town for 430 days and, when hungry, to cook his food over burning human poop. Fortunately, cooking over burning human poop happened to be Ezekiel's major in college.

God spoke to Hosea and commanded him to marry a prostitute who would repeatedly commit adultery and have children with other men. "Thank you, God; it's what I've dreamed of since I was a little boy!"

Saul was in the middle of searching for lost donkeys when God's messenger anointed him to be the first king of Israel. The idea of being king might sound like fun to us, but it wasn't a job Saul was interested in at all.

Little David felt led to take on a giant in a *mano y mano* battle.

Mary was an honorable virgin, pledged to be married, when God told her she would become pregnant out of wedlock. This, of course, would do wonders for her reputation.

The eleven remaining apostles after Judas's betrayal were all martyred for Jesus. Stephen gave a speech for Jesus that got him stoned to death. Paul was beaten and left for dead—repeatedly.

Seriously, who ever gets an assignment from God that sounds appealing? So where do we get the idea that God will ask us to do things we want to do?

Now there is some tension here. Because, as I mentioned earlier, God often calls us to the place where our "deep gladness" meets the "world's deep need." When God calls us, it will often be to a place of deep gladness—to something we're passionate and excited about. But it's also to the world's deep need, and that may make it dangerous, or difficult, or just a lot of work. And many decide it's easier to sit on our couches eating popcorn and watching *Shark Tank*—watching other people pursuing their deep gladness—while we take the easy path and miss out on life. God's plan for our lives is amazing, but it typically appears to be something we don't want to do.

This has been my story. I know people who feel like they're getting clear direction from God every day. I'm not that guy. But the times in my life when I knew God was speaking—it's *never* been what I wanted to hear. Leave your full scholarship and upcoming lucrative law career to accumulate big school loans at seminary and land a small salary. Leave a great church that is offering you a good deal to stay, and go to a church that has only eighty people and can't pay you anything. Leave the church that grew from eighty to over four hundred and can now pay you to start a brand-new church in a place you've never been. Leave the new church you started that has now become quite successful to start another brand-new church, this time in the stupidest place to start a church in America—just off the Strip in the heart of Sin City.

It's not just me; this is true of everyone who follows God's leading. When God speaks, it's just not what you want to hear. This year I spoke at a conference in which one of the other speakers was Ajai Lall.[1] Ajai is a missionary in India. He told stories about courageous Christians ministering in very dangerous areas. He talked about a time when two of his friends asked him to join them on a trip through India. They would go to different villages and towns and tell people about Jesus. Ajai joined them, and initially it went well. Then one night his friends said their next stop was Rajpura, a city of almost one hundred thousand people, none of whom were Christians, where Jesus had never been preached. They excitedly told him he'd be the first person to ever tell the people about Jesus, and that ten thousand posters had already been posted around the city announcing that Ajai Lall was coming to preach about Jesus.

What they didn't tell him was that Rajpura is a city where Islam extremists are trained and where Christians are not allowed to live. The one man who had previously tried to speak about Jesus there was killed.

They went to Rajpura, and the chief of police told them not to have their meeting. He explained that thousands of people were already marching in protest and that if the meeting happened, there would be a riot. Ajai's friend argued, "We live in a democratic nation. You can't stop us." The police chief conceded but said that to have the meeting they would have to sign a paper stating that if the meeting caused unrest, if the crowd got agitated, the police had permission to shoot the person speaking about Jesus. Ajai's friend said, "Give me the paper, I'm ready to sign it." Ajai said, "You're ready to sign, but I'm the one preaching. I don't know if I'm ready to sign!"

He called home and told his family about the situation, asking them what he should do. His children begged him not to preach there, but his wife told him that God wanted him to do this. "You need to preach," she said. "And you will preach the best message of your life. We will be on our knees."

They held the meeting outside, where anyone could come. Hundreds of extremists showed up, carrying guns and swords and iron rods. When it came time for Ajai to speak, the chief told five of his deputies to point their rifles at him. "When I give you the signal," he instructed, "shoot this man."

Ajai walked up to the mic and began explaining why Jesus is unique, why he is the only one who can give salvation. After forty minutes of speaking, he finished and sat down. When he did, the police chief said, "I have always hated Christians and hated Jesus, but now that I've heard the message, this is the message of life, of eternal life, of salvation, and hope!" They ended up starting a church in Rajpura, and that church has since started another church.

Ajai told another story about meeting with a group of Christians from a city in India where, in August of 2008, extremists set 285 church buildings on fire and killed two thousand Christians. One woman in the group was a widow of a preacher who had been killed in the massacre. She told Ajai about the night of August 23, 2008, when men burst into their house, tied her and her husband up, and made them watch as they raped their daughters. They then cut each of their daughters into three pieces, tied her husband to a huge rock, and threw him into a lake. Ajai sat in stunned silence, but the widow and all the others assured him that they were following God's will and were willing to suffer for it. A pastor in the group spoke for everyone when he said, "But we will not compromise. We will continue to share Jesus Christ, because people are dying who are lost without Christ. We will choose persecution instead of praise. We will choose harassment instead of honor. We will choose abuse instead of applause. We will choose death instead of dignity. Because we want to continue to live and be witnesses of our Lord Jesus Christ."

When You Hear God's Voice . . .

See, the question is not whether God speaks. He does. And it's not whether we can hear him. We can. The question is: Do we want to? Because when God calls, he leads us to dangerous places we're afraid to go. God calls us to embark on an adventure, to dare to dream big dreams, to take audacious risks.

And really, when you think about it, nothing else would make sense. We seek to minimize danger and to increase our level of comfort and chances of success, but living that life won't lead us to become the kind of people God wants us to become.

God wants us to have a vital reliance on him, and he wants us to form a deep bond with him through that dependence. But if we're playing it safe, we don't really need God. And so of course God is going to lead us to places we wouldn't dare to go on our own.

God wants us to be people who live lives of faith, and faith requires risk. If there is no risk, there's no faith required. Maybe we could say it this way: risk leads to fear, and our response to fear is faith. The other option, obviously, is to just live in fear. But God wants us to live in faith, and so when he speaks, he asks us to take risks. This is why the most repeated command in the Bible is "fear not." We all want to live risk-free, but God wants us to live free to risk.

God wants us to show the world how great he is, and how can the world see God's greatness in us if we only do what we can do on our own? I like how Henry Blackaby says this:

Some people say, "God will never ask me to do something I can't do." I have come to the place in my life that, if the assignment I sense God is giving me is something that I know I can handle, I know it is probably not from God. The kind of assignments God gives in the Bible are always God-sized. They are always beyond what people can do, because he wants to demonstrate his nature, his strength, his provision, and his kindness to his people and to a watching world. This is the only way the world will come to know him.[2]

Will You Obey?

God loves us and has a plan for our lives, but it's probably nothing like what we'd imagine. He calls us to risk, knowing that we'll experience fear, but hoping that we'll choose to live in faith.

What he tells us may not be what we want to hear, but it's *right*. And so when God speaks and tells us what to do, we need to trust him and obey.

We don't trust and obey because it will be awesome. It might be. It might not be. David followed God's plan and got to chop off Goliath's head. John the Baptist followed God's plan and got his head chopped off.

We trust him and obey.

If we're honest, we tend to view God like he's a genie in a bottle who exists to grant our wishes. If God is our genie in a bottle, and he asks us to do something we don't want to do, of course we won't obey. But if he is actually the sovereign God of the universe, and we've surrendered our lives to him, then we follow his leadership wherever it leads us.

We also know *God is love*. We know that God is not vindictive or capricious. We know that he is compassionate and caring and he really does have a good plan for our lives, even if that plan sometimes seems to make no sense. And when we obey, God's love becomes complete in us.[3] God's love is real all the time, but that doesn't mean we always *experience* God's love.

When we obey, we draw close to God and he draws close to us, and his love becomes real to us.

When God speaks, and we listen and obey, that's when the renegade adventure begins.

Let the Renegade Adventure Begin

Remember John Perkins and his wife, the couple God told to go to Africa? They were on a steamship traveling around the coast of Liberia when God whispered that this was to be their new home. But when they told the captain to bring them to shore, he refused because he knew if he did they would be eaten by cannibals.

Well, unbeknownst to the Perkinses, there was a young man living in that region named Jasper Toe. He believed there was a God, but had never heard the name of Jesus. One night he looked into the moonlit sky and thought, *If there is a God in heaven, help me find you.* And then he heard a voice. A voice he had never heard before. The voice said, "Go to Garraway Beach. You will see a box on the water with smoke coming out of it. And from that box on the water will come some people in a smaller box. These people in this small box will tell you how to find me."

It took Jasper Toe seven days to walk to Garraway Beach. He arrived on Christmas Day 1908. From the shore he saw what appeared to be a black box with smoke coming out of it, and it was floating on the water.

That was the moment John Perkins and his wife sensed God speaking to them, saying, "Get off the boat; this is your destination."

The captain refused their request, but they refused to take no for an answer. So John Perkins and his wife and all their belongings were put into a canoe, and they rowed to the beach.

When they arrived, Jasper Toe was waiting for them. He motioned for them to follow him, and they did. They walked in silence for days, back to his village, which became their new home. And the Perkinses learned the language. And the Perkinses led Jasper Toe to Christ. And together they started a church in that village. And, eventually, Jasper Toe started *hundreds* of churches in Liberia.[4]

And all of that happened because the Perkinses and Jasper Toe really did want to hear from God, and they were willing to obey no matter what he asked.

What about you?

16

Spend Your Time Waiting

I like to think of myself as a good cook. My main reason for believing this is that I watch *Top Chef*. I suppose watching an operation doesn't make someone a good surgeon, but c'mon, a boy can dream.

When I was in seminary, my then-girlfriend (and now wife), Jen, and one of our friends, Dan, drove about ten hours to see me. I decided I would show my appreciation by making them a turkey dinner. The only problem was that my only cooking experience was sticking frozen pizzas in the oven. Everything seemed fine until it was time for the turkey to be "done." I opened the oven only to find that it was actually "partially defrosted" after three hours in the oven! I put it back in and checked it an hour later—and decided it was now "mostly defrosted." At that point I announced my oven didn't work, and I brought the turkey down the hallway to my friend's apartment and put it in his oven. About two hours later Jen and I went to check the turkey and determined that it was now "done enough."

I started carrying it back down the hallway to my room when it happened. To this day I can't explain why or how. I guess it's possible I tripped. The turkey slipped, then the turkey fell, then the turkey hit the floor—then the turkey rolled. It started *rolling* down the hall. Up to that moment, I would have bet large sums of money that turkeys cannot roll, but it turns out they can and do.

At that point I thought about (1) crying, (2) laughing, (3) doing my best impression of Keith Jackson yelling, "Fummm-bbllle!" but instead what I actually did was . . . (4) I looked at Jen and said, "You listen, and you listen to me good. We are going to pick that turkey up, put it back in the pan, carry it to my room, walk in with big smiles on our faces, announce to Dan that the turkey is finally done, and we are going to eat this turkey. He is to *never* know it touched the ground, so we are not to clean it in any way. Yes, I realize this is a college apartment, and students walk this hallway in their bare feet, and most rarely shower, and I don't care! I made this turkey to show my appreciation for you and Dan, and after six hours of slaving over a hot* oven, you are going to eat it, foot fungus and all!"

It wasn't my greatest moment.

But it's exactly what we did. We picked up the turkey, brought it to the room, smiled, put it on the table, carved it, and ate it without saying a word to Dan, who died a month later of a strange bacterial infection.†

I bring all this up because I want you to think about two cooking-related things we have to consider if we're going to be renegades: cakes and microwaves.

Cakes

I have a long history with cakes. This may explain why I have a long history with being at least slightly overweight. When I

---

*The oven was actually pretty cold, but the "hot oven" comment felt right, and I was on a roll. And yes, I realize it's a miracle that she eventually married me.

†Dan did not actually die of a strange bacterial infection. But the rest of the story is true.

was fifteen I began working at a local grocery store. I continued working there throughout high school, and I ended up doing a little of everything. But one of my favorite jobs was making the huge sheet cakes people ordered for parties. I baked so many cakes for a stretch that I became able to break two eggs at a time, one in each hand. I was a finely tuned egg-breaking machine.

My favorite days were when people unhappily returned a cake because it wasn't done enough. I loved those days because we would suddenly have an entire sheet cake of slightly undercooked mushy cake perfection to eat all day.

Having made hundreds of cakes, I know that the stuff that goes into a cake is gross. When you make a cake, you get a bowl and you put in raw eggs, vegetable oil, flour, vanilla extract, and baking powder. You take all those gross-by-themselves ingredients and put them together. So how exactly do they end up becoming something so delicious? Well, there's one more ingredient. In fact, it's the magic ingredient (and no, it's not just the sugar):

Waiting.

You have to wait for the cake to cook. When you put it in the right amount of heat for the right amount of time, even though most of the stuff that goes into the cake *isn't* good, after you've waited, it's incredibly good.

I had no idea at the time, but that lesson I learned while making cakes carried profound theological weight, because the cake-making process is the same process God uses in our lives.

The Magic Ingredient

The issue is that God often tells us things we don't want to hear. And when we're willing to obey God, we're often selfishly motivated. We want the promised payoff. But the problem is that the promised payoff is often delayed. We have to wait.

Waiting is the magic ingredient God uses all the time.

God instructs us to wait at least forty-three times in the Old Testament alone.

> Wait for the LORD;
>   be strong and take heart
>   and wait for the LORD.[1]

> Be still before the LORD
>   and wait patiently for him.[2]

> Since ancient times no one has heard,
>   no ear has perceived,
> no eye has seen any God besides you,
>   who acts on behalf of those who wait on him.[3]

Abraham heard from God when he was seventy-five years old and childless. God spoke to him and promised that he and wife, Sarah, were going to have a child. In fact, they'd have so many descendants Abraham would be known as the father of a nation. Abraham must have thought, *Wait, I'm going to have sex again? It's been over ten years. Honey, break out the Viagra!* And Abraham must have expected Sarah to be pregnant the next day. After all, God had promised. But she wasn't. Nor was she the next week, or month, or decade. Abraham struggled through all kinds of doubt, and God reassured him that waiting was just part of his recipe. Finally, after *twenty-four* years, the pregnancy test came back positive.

God spoke to Joseph in a dream, making a promise to him that he would rule the land and have people bow down to him. So what happened next? Joseph was beat up by his brothers, sold into slavery, thrown in prison, falsely accused, sent back for more prison—and he waited. It turns out that waiting was the magic ingredient, because eventually he was made second in command of the most powerful nation in the world. People bowed to him.

It's not just the Old Testament. Waiting is in the New Testament as well. Think about Jesus, who waited to come to earth,

143

waited thirty years to start his ministry, waited three more years to do what he really came to do, and then waited three days till the resurrection. Even God himself, in human flesh, was not exempt from waiting.

Neither am I.

Neither are you.

God makes us wait.

Waiting is the magic ingredient God uses all the time. I love the way Christian ethicist Lewis Smedes puts it:

> Waiting is our destiny. As creatures who cannot by themselves bring about what they hope for, we wait in the darkness for a flame we cannot light. We wait in fear for a happy ending we cannot write. We wait for a "not yet" that feels like a "not ever." Waiting is the hardest work of hope.[4]

We have to wait, but Smedes is right: waiting is hard.

Later, when you're basking in victory, it's not so difficult to look back on the time of waiting, but when you're in the middle of it—yikes.

When I was in law school I met Jean, a member of the church I attended. Jean is a world-class athlete. Jean has set, and continues to hold, United States and world speed records in several events. Jean won a silver medal in the 1992 Olympic Games in Barcelona. I think that it would be pretty easy to convince Jean that there's waiting before victory. It would be no problem, because Jean has gotten through the waiting and experienced the victory.

I met another person who belonged to that same church named Ms. Driscoll, and she had a very different story. She was born with spina bifida, a disease where you have a hole in your spine. It impacts people differently; in Ms. Driscoll's case it affected her ability to walk, forcing her to use metal leg braces. Growing up, she was the object of ridicule from other kids. Unfortunately, she didn't have love or support from her family. They couldn't accept her handicap and were abusive to her both physically and emotionally. When Ms. Driscoll was in eighth grade, she was riding her bike when she took a turn too fast and crashed. She was rushed to the hospital, where it was discovered she had dislocated her hip. Doctors performed operation after operation to try to fix it. Finally, she was put in a body cast for over a year, in hopes that her hip would mend. After a year in a body cast, she had missed school the whole time and it was still dislocated. Because of her spina bifida, there wasn't enough muscle for her hip to heal.

So finally she was able to return to school, but now in a wheelchair that she would sit in for life. She was a fifteen-year-old girl with spina bifida and abusive parents who was a year-and-a-half behind in school and in a wheelchair that kept her from being accepted by her peers. She considered suicide, but there was one thing that kept her going: she did well in school and took pride in her grades. Finally she graduated from high school and entered college in Milwaukee to become a nurse, hoping to help others who had physical problems. Soon, however, her physical and increasing emotional problems became too much for her, and she flunked out of college.

So how do you tell Ms. Driscoll that yeah, all the ingredients are gross, but just wait, and there will be a cake at the end?

It's hard, especially if you're in the thick of waiting, but it's true. Yes, we have to wait, but waiting is the magic ingredient.

Microwaves

I think the problem is microwaves.

I come from a time before microwave ovens, an era when we counted cooking time in minutes and hours, never seconds. The funny thing is that this was just a couple of decades ago.

I remember when microwave ovens were rare and expensive. Finally we bought our first one and took home the odd, space-age machine. We were astonished by how fast it was. It was mind-boggling that we could heat up a bowl of soup in just a couple of minutes.

Today we get frustrated that microwaves don't cook quickly enough. We stare at the timer as it does its frustratingly slow march down to 0:00. We make comments about not having all day, and this popcorn better not burn.

I want my popcorn NOW!

And we're not just in a hurry when we make "home-cooked" meals in our microwaves, it's when we eat out too. There was once a land where drive-thrus didn't exist, but we can't imagine that. Having to get out of our car and sit down at a table to eat? How primitive! The truth is, drive-thrus are not quick enough for us now. If there are three or four cars in line, I'm just not having it.

I want my French fries NOW!

Or when we do go out to eat at a sit-down restaurant, like say on a Friday night at 6:30, we get angry if there's a thirty-minute wait. What exactly did we expect on a Friday night at 6:30? But still we drive up and send the runner in to see if there's a wait. Seriously? There are people sitting outside in the grass. One family has put up a tent. A guy built a fire. But you still send the kid in to find out if there's a wait. "What? Forty minutes! Ugh!"

Then comes my favorite line: "Let's go somewhere else where we won't have to wait."

I want my filet mignon NOW!

And it's not just food; it's *everything*. We're annoyed when the internet on our cell phones isn't fast enough. Read that last line again. We have internet on our phones! If you could go back in time just twenty years and tell someone that you have internet on your phone, they'd kill you in fear of your crazy spaceman talk. But we don't appreciate having access to everything in the world in our pocket, available in just seconds, because "just seconds" isn't fast enough.

I want to know what time the movie starts NOW!

Yes, we've been conditioned to expect things NOW.

My marriage needs to get better NOW! This diet better produce weight loss NOW! I know I just started this job, but I should get a promotion and a raise NOW!

And God? God needs to come through for me NOW as well. When I pray, I expect my prayers to be answered—not tomorrow, NOW! In the Bible, God promises me things like peace, joy, and hope, and I'd like all those things NOW!

But that's just not the way it works, especially not with God. God is cool with waiting, and with making us wait. As we go through life, many of the ingredients thrown into our bowls taste crappy, and if you're evaluating them NOW, you'll be disappointed. But if you can just be patient, you'll discover that waiting is God's magic ingredient.

All of that sounds good, but how do I tell that to Ms. Driscoll, this poor young lady stuck in a wheelchair with no friends and abusive parents? She just flunked out of college and is considering suicide. How do I tell her, "Don't worry, just wait. Because, after all, waiting is God's magic ingredient"?

It would be so much easier to tell Jean, the one setting records and winning Olympic medals.

But here's the thing: Ms. Driscoll is Jean.

Jean is Ms. Driscoll.

I lied. I said it was a "very different story," but it's actually exactly the same story.

In the midst of her depression and suicidal thoughts, Jean Driscoll heard about wheelchair racing and the phenomenal team they had at the University of Illinois. She went back to school in Milwaukee, got her grades up, and transferred to Illinois where she began to train and joined the team. Soon Jean Driscoll won the Boston Marathon for wheelchair racing. Then she did it again, and again, and again, each year breaking her own world record. She has several other world records and Olympic medals. She told her story when I was a part of her church, and said, "My wheelchair has been such a blessing to me." She shared all the amazing opportunities she's had to serve people and share God's love with them. God has her on an adventure and, according to her, it's all because of her spina bifida, her abusive parents, her bike accident, her wheelchair, and her flunking out of school. She said, "I'm so glad all that happened. I'm so glad."

But she wasn't glad when those things were happening. What she learned is that waiting is God's magic ingredient.

What to Do While You Wait

If we're going to live for God, we need to be patient. God calls us, and has an adventure for us, but in his wisdom he often moves more slowly than we'd like. So we need to get in sync with his timing and not get ahead of him. Saint Gregory said it well: "All holy desires grow by delay; and if they diminish by the delay, then they were never holy desires." And so we wait. We wait for the Lord, we're strong, and we take heart as we wait for the Lord.

But what do we do while we're in God's waiting room?

While we wait, we wrestle with God. The image we get in the Bible is that God is not afraid of tough questions. God understands when we struggle with doubts. God doesn't reject us for not being sure of his plan. God can handle it, and generally it's healthiest for us. If we stuff down our questions and doubts, they don't go away. Instead they often become toxic, growing into a bitterness that can even lead us away from God and his purpose for our lives. So while we wait, we're honest with ourselves and with God.

And while we wait, we embrace God. We seek his help and his strength. We look past our circumstances and we remember God's goodness and his promise, and that's where we put our faith and find our joy. This is exactly what Habakkuk did:

> Though the fig tree does not bud
>   and there are no grapes on the vines,
> though the olive crop fails
>   and the fields produce no food,
> though there are no sheep in the pen
>   and no cattle in the stalls,
> yet I will rejoice in the LORD,
>   I will be joyful in God my Savior.

148

The Sovereign LORD is my strength;
    he makes my feet like the feet of a deer,
    he enables me to tread on the heights.[5]

While we wait we wrestle with God, *and* we embrace God, believing that waiting is God's magic ingredient.

17

Break the Silence

What's the most overwhelming silence you have ever experienced?

I think back to times when I experienced the sound of intense silence.

The moment I realized my father was never coming back, our family was really going on without him, and I would be a person with divorced parents. Silence.

Or when I walked home from high school, after baseball practice, and went into the kitchen, where my mother looked at me and said, "Grandpa's dead." Silence.

Or the night when I was lying in bed with my wife and drifting off to sleep, when she whispered, "Vince, I don't like you." There were just no words to respond to that. The room just filled with silence.

How about you? Have you ever had a time when it was so silent the silence hurt your ears?

Your only hope was that the doctor would give the "right" diagnosis, but as he spoke you realized he was giving the wrong one. And then you just suffocated in the silence.

You got alone to pray, and the time had come. You needed an answer. God had to come through for you. He had to speak into your life. And so you prayed. You prayed heartfelt, earnest, desperate prayers. And then you listened. You listened with a real faith that God would say something. And then you sat in inescapable, heartbreaking silence.

Several years ago, while still living on the East Coast, I cautiously opened the door of my house and walked outside into the eye of a hurricane. Have you ever done that? The eye is the dead calm in the middle of the raging storm, and it is silent. Uncomfortably silent. Eerily silent. After standing there alone for a few minutes, I yelled. I shouted at the top of my lungs.

Sometimes you just have to break the silence.

Drift

Sometimes the reason you have to break the silence is because sometimes you drift from God.

That's exactly what happened to an entire group of people three thousand years ago.

The nation of Israel, even with its checkered past, had always been God's people.[1] But things had taken a downward turn. The nation had split in two. A succession of kings in each kingdom led the people on a path away from God. The northern kingdom hit rock bottom when Ahab became king. Ahab was the most contemptible in a long line of wicked kings.[2] He married a woman named Jezebel, a worshiper of Baal. She built a temple for Baal and employed 850 prophets of Baal and Ashtoreth (the supposed goddess-wife of Baal). Baal worship was evil. For instance, it included the sacrificing of infants. The Oriental Institute has excavated a temple of Ashtoreth from Ahab and Jezebel's time that contained a cemetery where they discovered many jars, each containing the remains of an infant. The prophets of Baal and Ashtoreth were official, state-licensed murderers of little children. In an attempt to lead the nation away from God and toward Baal,

Jezebel killed the prophets of God and forbade the Israelites to worship him.

Interestingly, Ahab and Jezebel's sons all had names compounded with *iah*, which is a contraction of God's name, Yahweh. This suggests that in some strange way Ahab still hung on to the religion of his childhood and thought of himself as a follower of Yahweh, despite the fact that he worshiped Baal, lived a perversely immoral life, and was married to a woman who despised God and his people.

The nation had followed Ahab's lead. They knew they were God's people. It was the identity handed down to them by their ancestors. They knew the stories of God and his people. They knew the right words to say about God. They had made commitments to God, and felt as though they were still keeping them. And so most did not overtly publicly deny God. They would have still claimed to believe in him *while* they worshiped Baal, lived immoral lives, and sought prosperity rather than holiness.

An entire nation of people who were supposed to have a relationship with God drifted away from him.

Elijah

Everyone, that is, except for Elijah. He was a renegade willing to fight against the current and continue to live for God alone.

Through Elijah, God confronted Ahab: because of the king's evil ways and the people's drifting from their devotion to God, it would no longer rain. It wouldn't rain until God made it rain.

This was more than just punishment; it was also a preemptive strike against Baal, who was believed to be the god of rain and storms. It was as if God was telling Ahab and the Israelites, "So you worship Baal, the god of rain? Well, I'm going to make it not rain. Pray to your Baal and see if he can produce a single drop."

And that's exactly what happened. It didn't rain for three years. Then God had Elijah confront Ahab again. Elijah explained to Ahab that he wanted to have a showdown with the 450 prophets of Baal. Ahab had to be thinking, *450 versus one? I'm liking those odds.* And then Elijah named the location: Mount Carmel. Mount Carmel was considered Baal's dwelling place. Ahab must have thought Elijah was smoking something. He was giving up home-field advantage. Ahab smiled and accepted the challenge.

The entire nation of Israel showed up at Mount Carmel to see the showdown. People jostled for places to sit with good visibility. Vendors made their way through the crowds, shouting, "Get your Mount Carmel Apples! Get your Mount Carmel Corn!" And then Elijah appeared. Across from him stood the 450 prophets of Baal.

Lllllet's get ready to rrrrrummmmblle!

Just before the battle began, Elijah stepped forward and motioned for the crowd to be quiet. Then he spoke these words: "How long will you waver between two opinions? If the LORD is God, follow him; but if Baal is God, follow him."[3]

The word translated "waver" is *pasha*. It can also be translated "dance." Elijah was speaking to the people of Israel, saying, "How long will you dance between two lovers? How long will you go back and forth between God and Baal, acting like somehow it's okay for you to live in relationship with both? If the Lord is God, follow him; but if Baal is God, follow him."

The crowd's reaction?

They said nothing.

Silence.

Thousands of people, all being stared at by Elijah while his question hung in the air. It had to be the loudest silence of all time, and their silence said everything.

They had been able to conveniently ignore the fact that they weren't faithful to their God, to their God who loved them and had always remained faithful to them. But now their spiritual adultery was being thrust in their faces. There was nothing they could say.

Have you ever been in that position? Have you ever found yourself drifting from God, from his love, from a relationship with him? Yet you did it with a sort of plausible deniability. Perhaps you continued to attend church. So how bad could it be? I mean, you were in church every week, and isn't that what counts?

Or you never stopped meeting with your Christian friends; you smiled and told them you were doing well and said that you'd pray for them, and isn't that what a faithful Christian says?

Or maybe you continued to do your "devotions." You took some time, almost every day, to read your Bible and say a few prayers, and isn't that the whole deal right there?

But the truth is, you were doing devotions but had lost your devotion. You were meeting with Christian friends, but not truly with God. You were present in church, but not living in God's presence.

There are husbands who give the appearance of having a great marriage but are having a series of affairs.

There are followers of God who give the appearance of having a great relationship with God and the whole time have another god on the side.

I've been one of them. I'm guessing you have too. Maybe you're there right now. And you've been able to do it without the guilt overwhelming you. You've been able to do it, and ignore that you're doing it, or find some way of justifying it. But right now your plausible deniability has been shattered, and perhaps your heart as well. You don't know what to say. There's really nothing you can say.

"The people said nothing."

Silence.

The Showdown

Elijah didn't get the response he had hoped for, so he set up the framework for the showdown. He told the 450 prophets of Baal to gather stones, build an altar for themselves, and pick two bulls.

Elijah instructed Baal's prophets to pick the bull they wanted, put it on their altar, and then do whatever was necessary to get Baal to respond with fire. Whichever god sent fire from heaven would be the true god.

The prophets of Baal loved this idea. Not only did Elijah give them home-court advantage, he had chosen a challenge that played right into their god's skill set. Baal was considered the god of rain, thunder, and lightning. If any god could bring down fire from heaven, it was Baal.

So they built the altar, prepared the bull, and started imploring Baal to bring the heat. They chanted. They sang. They even danced.

Here's the odd thing: Elijah did nothing. He sat and watched. It'd be like a football team in the Super Bowl not taking the field at opening kickoff, just letting the other team drive down the field without even trying to stop them.

By lunchtime the crowd had long stopped watching Elijah. At first it had been fascinating to see him not participate, but now it was just boring. Now they watched the 450 shouting, dancing, singing prophets, waiting for the moment when Baal would set the bull on fire.

And it's about this time that Elijah couldn't take it anymore, and he did something. He trash-talked. Perhaps the first historical account of trash talking happens in 1 Kings 18:27. One of the things he said about Baal was "maybe he's busy." Those words have been cleaned up a bit from the original for our delicate ears. Literally, Elijah said something closer to, "Maybe your god is busy . . . sitting on the toilet."*

Elijah gave it to them.

If you knew Hebrew (which Elijah spoke) and were there, you'd hear,

Yo' God is so dumb, it takes him two hours to watch *60 Minutes*.†

*That's true.
†That's not true.

155

Yo' God is so dumb, when he saw the "Under 17 Not Admitted" sign at the movie theater, he went home and got sixteen friends.*

Yo' God is so dumb, he thinks Fleetwood Mac is a new hamburger at McDonald's.†

Yo' God is so dumb, he spent twenty minutes staring at an orange juice container because it said, "Concentrate."‡

Elijah's trash talking provoked them to respond. How so? They pulled out their swords and spears and began ritualistically gouging and cutting themselves. Apparently this was an intense form of worship. They were offering their blood to Baal, trying to incite him to do something.

Now this may sound foreign to us, but I'm not so sure. *We've* turned away from God to false gods, little gods we hope will give what only God can give. If we're honest, *we bleed for those things*. We dream about them. Fantasize about them. We give ourselves to them. We offer them our time, our energy, our passion, our money.

We bleed for satisfaction.

We bleed for acceptance.

We bleed for meaning.

We bleed for our job.

We bleed for joy.

We bleed for fulfillment.

We bleed for the newest technology.

We bleed for a sense of belonging.

We bleed for our secret addiction.

We bleed for adventure.

We bleed for contentment.

*That's not true either. (They didn't actually have movie theaters back then.)
†Nope.
‡Not so much.

Here's the problem: the false little gods we've put our hope in never deliver. We're not that different from the prophets of Baal. We too shed our blood in the same desperate hope that the things we worship will meet our needs. And just like the prophets of Baal, we're left empty and increasingly desperate, because the only response we get is silence.

When you turn away from the one true God and give your attention to false gods, to little gods, the only answer you ever get is silence.

A Slap in the Face

Finally evening came, and Elijah had enough. He called the people to come closer, and they did. Elijah began to rebuild the altar. Notice, he didn't *build* an altar; he rebuilt *the* altar. There on Mount Carmel were the remains of an altar the Israelites had used for hundreds and hundreds of years to worship their God, but it had been unused for fifty years and was in ruins. So in front of the Israelites, Elijah carefully put back together the altar where they had made vows to their God.

The timing wasn't coincidental either. Elijah rebuilt the altar as the time for the evening sacrifice approached. The evening sacrifice was a sign of devotion that had been a part of the Israelites' worship. Well, it had been until the last fifty years. People had sort of forgotten about it.

Elijah gathered twelve big rocks to form the base of the altar. This was a slap-in-the-face reminder to the people gathered, who represented the twelve tribes of Israel, that they had broken their covenant to be faithful to God.

And when I put myself in the story, I realize that *I* need that slap in the face. I think back to worship practices that once kept me connected to God but I stopped doing years ago, sacrifices I used to make for God that I just don't seem to make anymore.

If I'm honest, I realize that there are ways in which I've grown and become a better person, but there are other areas in which

I'm just not the man I used to be, not the worshiper of God I used to be, and I need to rebuild some altars.

Maybe you do too.

Fire

Elijah finished rebuilding the altar, slaughtering the bull, and placing it on the altar. Then he made an unusual request. Actually, it's more of a command.

Elijah told the people to get water and pour it all over the bull and altar.

You can picture their objections.

"But Elijah, there's been a drought for three and a half years, a drought that we blame you for, by the way. So water is kind of in short supply."

"But Elijah, the competition you set up is that the true god needs to burn up the bull with fire. And so pouring water all over your bull, um . . . kind of counterproductive there, buddy."

Elijah said he knew that—just do it. And then Elijah told them to do it again. And then a third time. The bull and altar were soaking wet.

It's a, "Yo' prophet is so dumb, he poured water on the animal he wants to burn up" moment.

Elijah had stacked all the odds against himself and his God.

The prophets of Baal continued to shout and dance and sing and bleed, but still no fire. Not even a spark. Just silence.

Now Elijah was ready, and his timing was impeccable because it was now exactly the time for the traditional evening sacrifice. So finally, after an entire day of not asking God to do anything, Elijah stepped forward and prayed one simple prayer:

> Lord, the God of Abraham, Isaac and Israel, let it be known today that you are God in Israel and that I am your servant and have done all these things at your command. Answer me, Lord, answer me, so these people will know that you, Lord, are God, and that you are turning their hearts back again.[4]

And it happened.
Instantly.

> Then the fire of the LORD fell and burned up the sacrifice, the wood, the stones and the soil, and also licked up the water in the trench.[5]

We're not told what Elijah did in that moment, but I like to picture him looking over at all the stunned prophets of Baal, raising his eyebrows, and saying, "Who's your daddy?"

We *are* told how the Israelites responded:

> When all the people saw this, they fell prostrate and cried, "The LORD—he is God! The LORD—he is God!"[6]

Spiritual Adultery

Here's the question you and I have to wrestle with as we think through this story: Why was God so angry about what was happening in Israel?

You may think, *Well, duh, it was because the people were worshiping Baal instead of God.* But it wasn't.

The problem was that they were worshiping Baal AND God. God wasn't upset because they weren't worshiping him. He was upset because they were two-timing him. They were committing adultery by worshiping him while sneaking around behind his back and also worshiping Baal. We need to wrestle with that because we do the same thing.

We worship God. But at the same time, we have other things that we give the same attention, the same focus, and the same devotion—other things we value just as highly, if not more.

The truth is that *we're* Baal worshipers.

Maybe for you, the Baal you worship is the Baal of your body. You get up at holy-crap-how-early-is-it?!-o'clock every morning so you can spend an hour in the gym before work, or you go on three-hour runs on Saturdays, but you can't find fifteen minutes to talk to God. You count calories, infuse protein, and strain your cottage cheese to get out the one gram of milk fat, but you don't open your Bible. There's nothing wrong with being healthy, but maybe you're looking for something in your fitness, in your physical appearance, that you're supposed to look for in God alone. You've made your body into a god, into a Baal. And so Elijah's question comes to you: How long will you waver between opinions? If the Lord is God, follow him; but if Baal is God, follow him.

Or it could be that you worship the Baal of sex. Yes, God made us to feel attraction and sexual drives, but you're in overdrive. And so you look at things you would be ashamed for people to know you look at. You fantasize about people and would be mortified if they knew the thoughts that captivate your mind. Or maybe you're way past that and have decided that regardless of what God says about sexual purity, you're going to have sex with whomever you're going to have sex with. So you go to parties or bars on weekends, ignoring holiness and hoping for a hookup. The time has come for you to decide: How long will you waver between opinions? If the Lord is God, follow him; if Baal is God, follow him.

It may be that you worship the Baal of your job. Your devotion to your job matches or surpasses your devotion to God. So if your job requires you to do things that wouldn't please God, you'll do them, because that's what you have to do to get ahead. If your job demands hours that keep you from being involved in your church or serving your community, well, you have to do what you have to do. Maybe you hear stories of people who give up promotions because the time demands wouldn't allow them to live balanced lives, or who give up high-paying jobs to become pastors or missionaries, and it's beyond your ability to comprehend. So, how long will you waver between opinions? If the Lord is God, follow him; if Baal is God, follow him.

Your Baal may come in a bottle, or maybe you roll it and smoke it. You know your body is the temple of God, you've read the verse about not getting drunk, you know that if you were to truly live a life that honors God you'd go right now and flush your Baal down the toilet, but the thought freaks you out and you can't act on it. How long will you waver between opinions? If the Lord is God, follow him; if Baal is God, follow him.

Some of us worship the modern-day Baal of technology. The prophet who comes to you with the message from above has been Steve Jobs. Your obsession is how many Gs you can have on your cell phone, or getting the newest, flattest kind of flat screen. But are you obsessed with God? Not so much. And God is not pleased. The question comes to you: How long will you waver between opinions? If the Lord is God, follow him; if Baal is God, follow him.

In America, the Baal of choice for most is probably money. We worship it. I worship it. You worship it. And if you doubt that, you can determine your zeal for it by measuring your generosity with it. If you live in America, you are one of the richest people in the world. God has given you an abundance of money, and he has commanded you to share it. So how much do you give away? Ten percent is the minimum God allowed the Israelites to give. Do you even do that? I don't think giving the minimum can be called "generous," but if you're not at least giving the minimum God commands, you certainly can't say you're not worshiping money. So how long will you waver between opinions? If the Lord is God, follow him; if Baal is God, follow him.

Maybe the hard truth is that you *haven't* been a renegade.

You promised faithfulness to God, but you haven't been faithful. You know that only God can fulfill you, but you've been looking to other things. You've drifted from God to them, you've built altars to them, you've shouted and danced and sang for them. You've bled for them. But they haven't delivered, and they never will.

My prayer, like Elijah's, is that you would know today that the Lord is God, and you would turn your heart back to him.

What's your answer?

It's time to break the silence.

Your Renegade Assignment...
Should You Choose to Accept It

The crappy reality is that our sin will hold us back from fully living the rene-gade life, and so we need to allow God to free us from patterns of sin in our lives. How?

First, examine yourself and identify your sin patterns. The Bible teaches us to do this (see Lam. 3:40 and Ps. 139:23–24). If your areas of sin aren't imme-diately obvious, you might find clues to what they are in your resentments, your fears, or your strengths (our sins are often our strengths gone out of control). So what are your sin patterns?

_____

_____

Why do you think that particular temptation(s) is so alluring to you?

_____

_____

Now it's time to confess to God. Get raw with him. Be real and specific.

Next you need to repent, which means to turn away. Ask God to change your heart and for you to feel repulsed by what in the past has seemed attractive.

And now you need to develop a plan to allow God to free you from the sin pattern.

1. Pray every morning about it. Assume you'll be tempted, so prepare yourself.
2. Decide to play your life for an audience of One. From now on, it doesn't matter what anyone thinks but God. You will no longer cave because of peer pressure.
3. Memorize Bible verses that pertain to your area of temptation. When Jesus was tempted (see Luke 4:1–13), he responded to each tempta-tion with, "It is written" and then quoted a Bible verse. Why? Because temptation is a lie, and the antidote to a lie is the truth. We need to take our thoughts captive and replace lies with truth. Find Bible verses that represent the truth about your temptation and burn them into your

162

brain so you can say, "It is written." (Use a concordance or an online, searchable Bible like biblegateway.com, or ask your pastor to help you find verses. Then write the verses on a 3 x 5 card and carry it with you everywhere, looking at it repeatedly until it's tattooed on your brain.) So what verses will you commit to memory? (For instance, if your temptation is toward greed, you might memorize 1 Timothy 6:8; Matthew 6:19–21; and Philippians 4:13.)

_____

_____

4. Find a trusted friend to provide accountability. This needs to be someone who will pray for you and ask you consistently how you're doing with this particular sin, and whom you would call for support in a moment of temptation. So who will that person (or people) be?

_____

_____

18

Eat the Whole Burger

I never thought it would lead us into the bathroom. Worse, it was a public bathroom. There were several critical moments when we weren't alone. People watched me. They listened to me. But I couldn't stop. There was too much at stake.

The burger had to be eaten.

Let's start by turning the clock back half an hour.

As we walked into a new restaurant and saw a guy eating an enormous burger, I exclaimed something like, "Holy Hoochey Hamburger Heaven!" (I get excited easily.) Then, as we opened our menus, my son, Dawson, saw it. The challenge. Kids under twelve who ate a half-pound burger would get their picture on the wall. My nine-year-old son looked at me and said, with some apprehension, "I think I can do it, Dad."

His mother shook her head. "No, you're not."

I smiled. "Son, today is the day you're going to achieve glory."

I explained that he didn't have to do it, but if he started, he had to finish. "If you commit, you don't quit." He nodded nervously. I told him that I would do whatever I had to for him to reach the promised land of Burger Nirvana, describing how

164

Paul Newman as Cool Hand Luke had his stomach massaged as he ate fifty hard-boiled eggs. "I love you that much. I will massage the burger down your stomach if I have to."

He took a big first bite with a growl of determination. His next bites were followed by comments of how easy this would be and how they should make a tougher challenge. But not very far beyond a quarter pound he announced, "I'm done."

"I told you not to do it," said his mom.

"Why are you also having a milkshake?" asked his little sister.

"Meet. Me. In. The. Bathroom. Now," I commanded.

In the bathroom Dawson started giving silly, nine-year-old pansy excuses. "I'm too full. I ate a big lunch. Why didn't you tell me not to have a milkshake?"

I wasn't having it. "Remember hamburger glory? Remember the promised land? Remember if you commit, you don't quit?"

He wasn't having it. "Sorry, Dad. I'm done."

This probably should have been the first moment in Dawson's life when he realized the problem of having a pastor for a father, because I started preaching a sermon in the restroom.

"Dawson, I remember the first time I quit something. It was a baseball team, and to this day I wonder what would have happened if I didn't quit. Do you really want to have to live with that regret for the rest of your life?"

"It's just a hamburger, Dad."

I decided to give him Bible quotes. "Dawson, do you want to know what the Bible says?"

"No, Dad."

"It says, in Galatians 6:9, 'Let us not become weary in doing good, for at the proper time we will reap a harvest if we do not give up.'"

"I'm not 'doing good.' I'm doing a burger challenge."

"Do you want to know what else the Bible says?"

"No, Dad."

"It says, in James 1:12, 'Blessed is the one who perseveres under trial, because, having stood the test, that person will receive the crown of life that the Lord has promised to those who love him.'"

"I'm not under trial. I'm doing a burger challenge."

"Do you want to know what *else* the Bible says?"

"No, Dad."

"It says, in James 1:2–4, 'Consider it pure joy, my brothers and sisters, whenever you face trials of many kinds, because you know that the testing of your faith develops perseverance. Let perseverance finish its work so that you may be mature and complete, not lacking anything.' See, this is about perseverance!"

"I'm not facing a trial. I'm doing a burger challenge."

"No," I insisted, "this *is* a trial. It *is* about perseverance."

I decided to try nonbiblical quotes. "Persius said, 'He conquers who endures.' You need to endure so you can conquer this, and it will set you up for a life of conquering through endurance!"

I made up quotes. "Haven't you heard the quote: 'Perseverance is the path to greatness'?"

"No, Dad. Who said that?"

"Um, well, I did! I just did, right here. That's a brand-new quote! And you know new is always better!"

I tried poetry. "Dawson, Nelson Mandela faced seemingly insurmountable odds when he was imprisoned because of the color of his skin. And in jail he was inspired by a poem. How does it go? Um, 'In the fell clutch of circumstance, I have not winced nor cried aloud. Um, under the bludgeoning of change, my head is bloody, but unbowed. Beyond this, um, um, well, yada, yada, yada, I am the master of my fate.' Doesn't that inspire you to get out of . . . burger prison . . . and finish the challenge?!"

"I guess a little."

I told him the story of how Dr. Martin Luther King Jr. stared into the hateful eyes of racism and oppression, and he never gave up, he endured. "Dawson, can't you stare into the beefy eyes of that 10 percent of a pound of burger and tell it that you will not go quietly into that dark night?"

"What are you talking about, Dad?"

"I'm talking about free at last, free at last, finish that burger, and you'll be free at last."

Blank stare.

Finally, I pulled out the big guns. Winston Churchill. There was a guy in the bathroom with us, but I didn't care. I was not going to allow my son to quit. So I told him of Churchill's short but amazing speech where he said only six words, "Never, never, never, never give up." I described how Churchill removed his shoe and smacked it against the podium as he spoke. As I did, I took off my sneaker and pounded the sink for effect.*

It worked!

Dawson said, "Dad, you're right. I can do this. I can do this!"

And he bolted out of the bathroom and triumphantly finished the burger. And, praise Paul Newman, I didn't even have to massage his stomach while he did it.

When a Burger Isn't a Burger

I may have gone a little overboard, but I still believe the difference between someone who quits and someone who perseveres is *everything*. And as I made up in the bathroom that wise sage said in the past, perseverance really is the path to greatness. And I want my son on that path. *I* want to be on that path. And I want *you* on that path.

Once we commit to living fully for God, we need to persevere and continue to the end. We'll always be tempted to quit on the renegade life, but we can't quit. In what ways have you already quit? I wonder where you haven't endured, and what might have been. What might've happened if you didn't . . .

- stop going to church?
- quit on your marriage?
- stop reading your Bible every day?
- give up on your dream of being a missionary?

*Yes, history buffs, I know it wasn't Winston Churchill but Nikita Khrushchev who pounded his shoe on the podium, but it seemed like a winning move to use on a nine-year-old.

- quit on your diet?
- drop out of college?
- stop meeting with your accountability friend?
- give up on praying intense, needy prayers?
- quit serving in that ministry at church?
- stop believing God could do anything with your life?

We don't know the answers, because we didn't endure.

But what might happen if we start? What if today becomes the day we decided to live with persistence?

And you could. Trust me, you could do this. You and God together could *totally* do this. (And if you doubt that, I would love to take you into the bathroom for a little motivational speech.) And as you do, as you develop persistence, it will put you on the path to greatness.

The Path to Greatness

What separates average people from amazing people is not their talent or intelligence. It's not who they know or what they know—it's persistence.

This is really good news for you and me. It means it's okay if you're not talented. It's not a problem if you don't know the right people. It's not the end of the world if you're not educated. You can still live an amazing life for God, if you . . .

- just keep putting one foot in front of the other
- won't take no for an answer
- make another call
- say another prayer
- write another check
- attend another class
- send another email
- memorize another verse

- continue to dream that dream
- attend another session with your counselor
- make it through another day of sobriety
- talk again with your teenager
- just don't quit

We see this in every arena of life.

Sports. The most amazing athlete of my lifetime? Michael Jordan. Was it easy for him because of his enormous talent? Well, Michael Jordan was actually cut from his high school basketball team. He wasn't good enough. So no, it wasn't easy. He could have decided to quit. But instead he chose to persevere.

Entertainment. The most amazing band of my lifetime? U2. So was it easy for them because of their enormous talent? Well, U2 actually did so poorly starting out that they couldn't afford their third world tour and had to put all of it on their manager's credit card. He ended up losing that credit card because U2 wasn't making enough for him to afford the payments. It wasn't easy. They could have decided to quit. But instead they chose to persevere.

Business. The most amazing business leader of my lifetime? Steve Jobs. So was it easy for him because of his enormous talent? Well, Steve Jobs founded Apple Computers, and then got *fired from* Apple Computers. It wasn't easy. He had to fight for twelve years to take back over the company he had started. He could have quit. But instead he chose to persevere.

We see this in every arena of life, but the place I think we see it most vividly is in the kingdom of God. What separates people who live average lives for God from those who live amazing lives is *perseverance*.

I've done a series at church every few years called World Changers where we look at the lives of people who have had a remarkable impact for God. I've noticed there seems to be a theme that runs through the lives of all these heroes of our faith. For instance . . .

John Wesley was born in 1703, the fifteenth of nineteen kids. They grew up extremely poor.* When John was six years old their home burned down and he barely escaped. Later in life John Wesley became a preacher. And as a result of his preaching, he was beaten up regularly. He had bricks thrown at him. His horses were poisoned. He was stoned. The churches of his day thought his call to discipleship was too extreme, so no one would let him preach. So Wesley began preaching out in fields, and people came to hear him by the thousands. He had a worldwide and enduring impact through starting churches and training up pastors. But it wasn't easy. He could have decided to quit. But instead he chose to persevere.

William Carey was not someone you'd expect to live an amazing life for God. He was an ordinary shoemaker in England in the 1700s. He and some friends got together every week to pray for the nations, and repeatedly Carey felt God calling him to India. So . . . he and his family moved to India. The impact William Carey had there was unbelievable. He's known as the "father of modern missions." His work led to the starting of hundreds of churches, with thousands of people coming to faith in Jesus. At that time in India wives were often burned alive on their husbands' funeral pyres as an offering to the gods, and children were sacrificed at a yearly festival. Against tremendous opposition William Carey fought zealously against these horrible practices—and won. To this day the statute criminalizing infanticide is called the Carey edict. But it wasn't easy. In his family's first year in India one of their children died. Carey's wife became so depressed she nearly lost her mind. Soon, she died. He was now left alone to raise two children in a foreign land. Yet he kept going, but without seeing results. In fact, not a single person came to Christ. Confusion and despair swept over Carey, but he refused to quit. He began translating the Bible into different Indian languages. Then the building with his printing

---

*I suppose if you decide to have nineteen kids, there are consequences. If you want some extra spending money, maybe try staying out of the bedroom.

press and vital translation work burned to the ground. So what did he do? He started over. He could have decided to quit. But instead he chose to persevere.

Adoniram Judson is one of the people who followed Carey's lead and decided to move to India in the 1700s, though he ended up in Burma, where he established sixty-three churches and personally led over six thousand Burmese to faith in Christ. But it wasn't easy. Judson was a twenty-two-year-old American when he made the initial decision to go to India, but when he arrived at the port they would not let him in. He could have gone back home, but he told his pregnant wife that they would go to every port in India until they found one that would let them in. So they went back out into the Bay of Bengal, and a monsoon hit. For three weeks they were stuck at sea. Judson's wife gave birth on that boat, in that storm, and their baby died. Finally the Judsons were allowed to land in a dirty little town called Rangoon, not in India but in Burma. Judson began sharing Christ, and did so every day for over six years, but not one person came to Christ. His financial supporters in America wrote him, urging him to quit and telling him that they would no longer be sending financial support. He could have gone back home, but he stayed. Soon the Rangoon authorities tired of his preaching so they put him in jail. Judson spent *years* in jail, chained, with his back, shoulders, and head on the ground and his legs up in stocks against the wall. At one point he spent two years straight in that position. He slept in that position. He ate in that position. He went to the bathroom in that position. (And he translated the entire Bible into Burmese in that position, hiding it in his pillow when the guards came in.) His wife and all three of their children died in Burma. He married again and had two more children. They also died in Burma. It was anything but easy. He could have decided to quit. But instead, he chose to persevere.

Dietrich Bonhoeffer was a youth pastor and college professor in Germany in 1933 when the Nazis took over. Many Christians in Germany decided to follow Hitler rather than Jesus, some because they were pressured to do so. In fact, most of Bonhoeffer's Christian friends became supporters of Hitler. Bonhoeffer refused. He decided to stand up for the oppressed Jews, but no one would listen. He decided his message might have more impact outside his country, so he moved to London, where he began pastoring two churches. But back in Germany, Hitler's power was growing and churches and seminaries were being taken over by the Nazis. As an act of allegiance to Hitler, German church leaders began taking a stand against Bonhoeffer. The Nazis threatened to kill him. So guess what Bonhoeffer did? Well, he quit, right?

No. He moved back to Germany. It was a crazy move, but that was where he felt he was needed most. Soon he was arrested for helping Jews escape to Switzerland, and then again for taking part in a plot against Hitler. Bonhoeffer spent two years in prison, where he wrote books that are still having a powerful impact around the world today. Then, on April 9, 1945, he was stripped naked and had a noose put around his neck. His last words were, "This is the end. For me, the beginning of life." And he was hung. It wasn't easy for Bonhoeffer. He could have decided to quit. But, instead, he chose to persevere.

Perseverance is the path to greatness.

Why Do We Quit?

Why do we quit? No one starts with the idea of giving up, so why do we end up doing it? Why do we miss out on greatness?

I suppose there are lots of reasons. One is that *we give ourselves the option of quitting*. I think half the reason so many marriages end in divorce is because the couple allowed for the possibility of divorce. Couples who don't consider it an option fight through the difficulties and figure out how to make their marriage work. Couples who consider bailing an option when the difficulties seem unbearable can just quit. And it's not just marriage. I've had diets I committed to 100 percent and never quit. I've had diets that seemed like a good idea and lasted a week. I've started and stopped writing several books, but when I've had a book contract and a due date, I've never even considered giving up.

We'll quit if we give ourselves the option of quitting.

I've realized that I can't be 100 percent committed to everything, so I've spent some time determining where quitting is not an option in my life. I've had to ask: Do I need to be 100 percent committed to . . .

- my wife?
- my kids?
- my extended family?
- my favorite sports teams?
- God?
- God's specific calling on my life?
- the specific church I'm serving?
- watching *American Idol*?
- my health?
- reading and continuing to learn and grow?
- my friends? Which friends?
- getting and staying out of debt?

I've made a decision on whether each of these requires life-long endurance. For those that do, I've tried to clarify what success looks like and what might constitute quitting, because it's simply not an option.

A second reason we quit is that *it's hard*. What's hard? *It* is, whatever *it* is. If *it* is something designed to help us grow as people, improve a relationship, or increase our impact on the world, *it* is going to be hard. The path to greatness is never smooth but is always a difficult journey over rough terrain. And so, if we've given ourselves the option of quitting—when things get hard, we will.

If you decide to be a renegade for God, you are going to have moments when it's difficult, when you start experiencing turbulence, or when God doesn't seem to be coming through. You decide to . . .

- go on a mission trip, but the money you need to raise doesn't come in as you expected.
- lose weight and get in shape so you can honor God with your body, and there are two birthdays at work in the same week so the break room is filled with cake.
- volunteer in your church's children's ministry, but a parent gets upset with you for something that isn't even your fault.
- improve your marriage by going to counseling, but your spouse refuses.
- share your faith with your friend, who then proceeds to verbally attack you for what you believe.
- get out of debt and live on a budget, and the next day your car breaks down and you don't have enough money for the repairs.
- serve in your church on Sunday mornings, but then something goes wrong every week that makes it almost impossible to get there on time.

None of that should take you by surprise. It always happens that way. *It* is always hard.

I'm trying to live a life where I have intimacy with God and influence on the world. Well, I have issues with intimacy. I've had a counselor diagnose me as having attachment disorder. Attachment disorder is when a person has harmful experiences in childhood and, in a very real sense, closes off his or her heart to avoid future pain. As I understand it, brain scans on people with this disorder show black holes of inactivity where there should be activity. People with attachment disorder find it difficult or impossible to form intimate relationships.

174

I've had another counselor diagnose me as having ADD. People with ADD have trouble focusing and their minds are easily distracted. Can you picture trying to have a time of focused, uninterrupted prayer with God that leads you into intimacy with him when you have attachment disorder *and* ADD? Welcome to my life. It's *hard*. And God has called me to have influence by being a pastor who starts churches for people who don't believe in God and hate church. I'm an introverted pastor trying to connect with people who don't want to connect with a pastor. It's *hard*.

It's hard for me, and it will be hard for you. It's always hard. And hard is why we quit. But from now on, you're not going to quit—because you've made the decision not to give yourself that option.

A third reason we quit is because *we can't see the future*. Perseverance is the path to greatness. People who persevere endure difficulties because they're looking forward to the reward that awaits, a reward that is unseen but considered certain.

There was an American swimmer named Florence Chadwick who became famous for being the first woman to swim the English Channel both ways. She then set another swimming goal, and on July 4, 1951, started her swim from Catalina to the California coastline. Unfortunately, she didn't quite make it. What stopped her? It wasn't the cold water, or sharks, or exhaustion from the sixteen-hour swim. What stopped her was fog. Fog rolled in and Chadwick could no longer see the coastline, and so she quit. When she climbed in the boat she discovered she was less than one mile from her goal. She later said, "If the fog hadn't been there and I could have seen the land, I would have made it." In fact, two months later she made a second attempt, and this time was different. Not because there was no fog. The fog was even thicker that day. So what was the difference? She said that she kept a mental image of the shoreline in her mind the entire time she swam.

We quit because we can't see the future. But people who persevere look forward to the rewards of greatness.

A fourth reason we quit is because *we don't realize we are always training ourselves to either become quitters or to become people who persevere*. The reality is that every time we quit, it becomes easier to quit the next time. When we fight through difficult circumstances and endure, we discover our own strength, we learn to rely on God, our self-esteem grows, and it becomes easier to endure the next time.

That brings us back to the restaurant bathroom. I didn't care if my son got his picture on the wall for his great achievement in gluttony. He actually would've been physically healthier if he had quit. But he also would have taken a step onto the path of quitting. And you know what ~~I always say~~ a great thinker said: quitting is the path to mediocrity. I had to use that burger challenge to teach my son he's better than that. He could endure. He could see the future and start to taste the reward of victory. (Which might be difficult through all that ground beef.)

So what about you? How are you currently tempted to quit? Don't do it.

Perseverance *is* the path to greatness.

19

Go Out in a Blaze of Glory

was sitting on a bed in a Las Vegas casino, crying because of what I had just done. I didn't want to spend my life full of regrets, but after what had just happened in that bed, I could now see it stretching out before me.

What had I done?

Well, I was alone in that hotel room. In fact, I had been by myself for a couple of days. And what I had done was a spiritual retreat.

Why in a casino? Well, I had asked my wife to find me a place where I could be by myself for a few days, and she booked me a room in a casino in the next town over from us. "Really?" I asked. "For a spiritual retreat?" She explained that it was the least expensive room she could find. (We are very cheap people.)

My sole purpose for this retreat was to discover my *soul* purpose. I wanted to come to a fuller understanding of my life's mission.*

---

*In The Renegade Life Plan appendix I have explained the process I used during that retreat to construct my life map.

I started this journey of discovery by focusing on the end of my life's journey. I imagined my funeral. I visualized a church, a coffin, pictures of me, flowers, and people filing in and finding places to sit. At one point in the service, people were given the opportunity to speak. My wife, my son, my daughter, and some close friends each walked up to the podium. What would they say? What would they remember about me? What impact would I have had on their lives?

Thinking it through, actually visualizing it, and imagining the words they might say left me in tears, because I knew someday this fantasy would be reality.

Someday each one of us will be in a box underground. We can think of that as a morbid reality we prefer to ignore, or it can be a reality that changes everything for us.

About Who?

In *About Schmidt*, Jack Nicholson plays Warren Schmidt.[1] The movie opens with Warren sitting silently in his barren corporate office, watching the wall clock's second hand lurch around its face. Boxes are stacked along one wall, waiting to be hauled downstairs as Warren Schmidt placidly waits for the final moments of his career to expire. He's been an actuary (a risk evaluator) for an insurance company for thirty years. As he sits in his office chair, it's almost as if he's trying to feel something but can't. He leaves and makes his way to a meaningless retirement dinner, and then to his house with his wife, Helen. At home he looks at his wife of forty-two years and asks himself, "Who is this old woman who is in my house?"

She could ask a similar question about him. They've lived dutiful and obedient lives, he as an actuary, she as a housewife, and now that the corporate world has discarded them, they have no other roles to assume. In fact, Warren soon makes his way back to his old company to see if he can answer any questions the new guy who took his place might have, but the new guy has none. In a lifetime of work, Warren Schmidt hasn't

178

accumulated even one piece of information that is needed by his replacement.

Warren begins a life of sitting in front of his television and eating sandwiches and potato chips. One day he sees a commercial for a children's charity, and he decides to "adopt" a six-year-old Tanzanian named Ndugu by sending a check for thirty dollars a month. His lonely, boring life of quiet desperation continues.

The movie is billed as a comedy, but it's really more of a tragedy. One of the few comedic elements is that Warren receives a letter encouraging him to write to Ndugu. Warren begins writing odd, detailed letters to this little Tanzanian boy, who would know nothing of American life. But the irony is that Warren knows nothing of American life either. We watch a moment from Warren's life, and then we hear his clueless, oblivious, aggrandized account of it in a letter to Ndugu.

Warren and Helen had purchased a thirty-five-foot Winnebago Adventurer so they could spend their retirement out on the road, seeing the world, but soon after his retirement Warren's wife drops dead in their kitchen. Warren is surprised—not at the enormity of his loss but that he had so little to lose. Upon going through her things, Warren discovers that years earlier she had had an affair with his best friend.

Warren and Helen had one child, a daughter who lives in Denver and is about to marry a waterbed salesman whom Warren feels is a "nincompoop." So after much inner turmoil, Warren hits the road in his RV to dissuade his daughter from her marriage plans.

When Warren finally arrives in Denver, he has no luck in stopping the wedding and realizes he has a superficial, strained relationship with his daughter. So Warren gets back in his RV and returns to Omaha, to his empty house and his empty life. He walks into his home, realizing that his life has amounted to nothing.

Warren enters his home completely depressed and goes through the stack of mail that built up while he was away. He notices an envelope from Tanzania and opens it. Inside is a letter from a nun where Ngudu lives, and she explains to Warren how his checks have made such a difference in Ngudu's life. He now has food to eat, and he can read, and on and on. And as he reads this, Warren Schmidt falls apart, sobbing uncontrollably, because he realizes he made a difference. Maybe his life was a waste, perhaps his marriage was a sham, he may have no real relationship with his daughter, but at least he made a difference in the life of one six-year-old boy from Tanzania.

About You

Here's the deal: there's a story being written about you, about your life, and it's being written by you. Someday that story is going to come to an end. When that day comes, you can look back like Warren Schmidt, realizing all the things you *didn't* do, choking on regrets, desperately grasping at the few good things you accomplished to make you feel a little better about your wasted life.

Or you can go out in a blaze of glory like a renegade.

Renegades don't have much remorse when they look back at their lives. Sure, they go through some tumultuous times, experience some discouragement, maybe wish they had trusted God a little more. But they've lived the life of a renegade, walking alone in faith when necessary, being poured into by God and poured out for him, and taking risks for him. You can have that, but to end your life that way, you need to start today.

The problem is that we tend to put off the important things. Warren Schmidt waited till the end to do anything worthwhile. You don't get to your destination in a day. It's a journey of a million steps, and each day we need to take another step in the direction of our destiny. Each day we don't is a day we walk away from our dreams.

If we wait for too many tomorrows, eventually it's too late. Warren Schmidt took one right step, and it helped one child, and that is touching. It was supposed to give the audience warm, fuzzy feelings, but I just wasn't satisfied. He lived an *entire life* and had *one* thing to show for it?

It's just not enough. The irony of the movie is that Warren Schmidt was an actuary, a risk assessor, and he never took a risk his entire life! And if you'll allow it, let me be an actuary for you: the most risky thing you can do with your life is *nothing*. The greatest risk is to get to the end of your life and have nothing to show for it. That's a risk you don't want to take. Turning away from the idols you've treasured, taking a stand for God, going every week to feed homeless people, signing up to help a kid, sharing your faith with a friend at work, volunteering in your church's children's ministry, being really vulnerable with a friend, giving God at least 10 percent of your income, moving to Africa to be a missionary for the rest of your life—those things may sound risky, but they aren't risky at all compared to doing nothing.

You were made to spend your life in a risky partnership with God. God placed you on this earth to live in intimacy with him and to have influence for him. You can live that way. And when you die, you can go out in a blaze of glory.

About the Renegades

Necati Aydin was weary from ten days of traveling. He didn't want to get out of bed, and his wife just wanted him to stay home. But Necati had a mission: he was trying to turn the world upside down. The corner of the globe God had given him was the Muslim nation of Turkey, where less than 1 percent of the people follow Jesus. So he got out bed and prepared for the day. When he reached the office, he discovered that his two ministry partners had five visitors who said they were interested in learning more about Christianity. But they lied. They quickly took out guns and knives and told Necati to convert to Islam and confess to them, "There is no God except Allah, and Muhammad is his prophet." Necati refused, and the cutting began. Necati and his two friends were tortured for an hour. Finally the police arrived and began pounding on the door. The attackers then sliced the throats of Necati and his two partners, and the last word heard by the police from the other side of the door was the passionate cry of a resolute Christian: "Messiah! Messiah!"[2]

When Necati died, he went out in a blaze of glory.

It's important to realize that Necati didn't have any more resources to live for God than you and I have. He wasn't born with a special obedience or martyrdom gene. He simply decided, each day for a long time, to live a dangerous life for God, seeking God's help along the way. That's all. And we are all capable of doing the same.

We are as capable, for example, as Father Damien of Hawaii.

Kalaupapa is one of the most beautiful parts of Molokai, which is one of the Hawaiian islands. It was once home to a leper colony. In the 1840s cases of leprosy started to break out in Hawaii, and the government segregated all with the disease to Kalaupapa.

Father Damien was a priest serving in Hawaii when, in 1873, at the age of thirty-three, he wrote his superiors, "I want to sacrifice myself for the poor lepers." They eventually said yes. He moved to Kalaupapa, and for sixteen years poured out his life serving them, loving them, and burying them. He learned their language, organized schools, bands, and choirs, built homes for them to live in and coffins for them to be buried in, and always spoke to them of the love of God. He became one of them. He became a leper, not only metaphorically through his friendship to them but eventually literally. One day he began his sermon with the words, "We lepers," and everyone realized that they were now truly in it together. He had chosen to live as they lived, and now he would die as they died. Father Damien did so at the age of fifty-five.[3]

When Father Damien died, he went out in a blaze of glory.

It's what renegades do.

About a Duck God

Philosopher Søren Kierkegaard told what he called the story of the duck god. It's the story about a duck world, where everyone is a duck. Since everyone is a duck, when they refer to God they call him the duck god. All the ducks would go to church on Sunday. The duck preacher would get up and say, "The duck god is a mighty god." And all the ducks would shout their agreement, "Quack, quack, quack!" (If you're in a private place, you might want to try it, because it feels pretty good. Let out a hearty, "Quack, quack, quack!") The preacher said, "So the duck god is a mighty god!" "Quack, quack, quack!" "And this duck god has created you with wings." "Quack, quack, quack!" "And he's created you with wings for a purpose, so that you can fly!" "Quack, quack, quack!" "And when you use those wings, you are going to experience a freedom that you never experienced before!" "Quack, quack, quack!" "So I'm going to challenge you, use those wings!" "Quack, quack, quack!" "Use them mightily!" "Quack, quack, quack!"

Here's the tragedy: when the service was over, everyone waddled home.

You can finish this book and conclude, "That was a good book," or maybe "That book wasn't so great," or you can realize that what matters is not the quality of this book but the quality of your life.

God matters.

Your life matters. And one day your life will be over.

So take this book and *apply it.* Say yes to God's call to become a renegade who lives dangerously.

Don't waste your life. Live it. Live it in a dangerous partnership with God.

(Quack, quack, quack!)

Acknowledgments

I want to thank:

Jesus: the original Renegade, and the One to whom I owe everything.

My wife, Jennifer: I couldn't do any of this without you. Thank you for being my renegade life partner.

My kids, Dawson and Marissa: I have the greatest kids in the world, and my greatest prayer is that you'll grow up to live dangerous, risk-taking lives for Jesus because of your love for God.

Verve Church and Forefront Church: it's been an honor to be your pastor. Thank you to all the renegades who allow me to see what all of this looks like in real life.

And all the people who helped me bring this book to life: Aaron Saufley, Nikki Brungard, Cherie Roe, Gilbert Thurston, Rebecca Cooper, and especially Chad Allen, Lindsey Spoolstra, and the whole team at Baker Books.

The Renegade Life Plan

What would it look like for you to live a renegade life and someday go out in a blaze of glory?

I don't know, but I do know it doesn't just happen. People don't meander into a meaningful existence. The Bible warns us in Psalm 90, "You sweep people away in the sleep of death—they are like the new grass of the morning: In the morning it springs up new, but by evening it is dry and withered."[1] Life is short, and one day we'll be the one in the box, so what should we do? We're told, "Teach us to number our days, that we may gain a heart of wisdom."[2]

To live the life we want, we need to live life by design. If you're the spontaneous, freewheeling type, that thought might turn you off, but just do this anyway. You can be spontaneous in all kinds of ways, but there are some critical factors of your life that require intentionality. Gary Kasparov dominated the chess world for several decades. In his book *How Life Imitates Chess*, he writes, "A Grandmaster makes the best moves because they are based on what he wants the board to look like ten or twenty moves in the future."[3] People who are masters at life know what they want their lives to look like ten or twenty years in the future, and they live today in a way that will get them there.

So how do you construct a plan? There are all kinds of "systems" you can find in blogs and books, but this appendix will get you started, and it's basically what I did in that casino hotel room.

Putting this plan together will be difficult, time consuming, emotional, and worth it. Many people find that generating this kind of plan is the key that allows them to move forward and start living the life they've always wanted to live.

We'll break this plan into seven bite-size chunks. Set aside a little time each day for the next week, do the work, and you'll be rewarded with a life-changing plan to help you become a renegade.

Day One

Creating Your Plan

Picture your life as a journey, almost like a road trip. Your goal, of course, is not to arrive at random destinations but to live in a way that will get you where you want to go. Your answers to some critical questions will come together to create a plan that will help you determine and reach your destinations.

Question One: How does your life break up into different journeys?

Everything in your life is integrated, but for our purposes it will help you to divide your life into different journeys. So what are the important journeys you are currently on? My list has eight different journeys: God, Character, Health, Finances, Wife, Kids, Friends, and Ministry. Those are the "categories" of my life that are important to me. You may add your career, or a hobby you're passionate about, or the hundreds of orphan Guatemalan toy poodles you've adopted.

Take some time to make a list of your life journeys.

188

Day Two

Question Two: What destination do you want to arrive at for each journey?

This is where the imaginary funeral comes in. In this step you're visualizing what your life would look like if it came out right. What do you want your spouse, kids, and friends to be able to (honestly) say about you? In what ways will you want to have served God and have made an impact in the world? In what kind of shape do you want to be in both financially and physically? What do you hope to accomplish in your career?

When you write this, write in the present tense, as if these destinations are your current reality, even if they're not. That way each time you read this, it will help you to imagine what it will feel like when you reach each destination.

So, for instance, here is the destination I wrote for my relationship with my kids:

> I am an example to Dawson and Marissa of what it looks like to radically love God and love people. They know that I don't love perfectly, but I don't pretend to, and my passion for wanting to love God and people, and my authenticity about it, allows them to follow my example.
>
> I love my kids unconditionally, and they are secure in that. But I love them too much to not help them become more like Jesus. So I lovingly encourage them to completely live their lives for him.
>
> I believe in my kids and I am their number one fan. I do everything I can to help them become everything God has in mind for them, and to accomplish the dreams he puts in them.
>
> I am always available to my kids and they know it. I make time for them so we're together a lot. We plan and do lots of special things together. I am fun to be around, and they want to be with me.
>
> Together we are living dangerous lives of faith because we follow Jesus, and he leads us to places we'd never dare go without him. We do it gladly because we're willing to do whatever it takes to follow Jesus and help others to know him.

Take some time to prayerfully write the destination you want to arrive at for each of your life's journeys.

Day Three

Question Three: How does that destination translate into specific, measurable goals?

You'll find it helpful to translate each of your destinations into some specific, measurable goals.

For some of your journeys, this will be complicated. For instance, it might be difficult to make specific, measurable goals for your relationship with God or with your spouse. For other journeys, perhaps your health or finances, it will be relatively easy to create goals.

Even if it's difficult, you'll find it helpful to translate your destinations into goals because your plan will become more concrete. It will feel less like a hazy, feel-good dream and more like something you can take steps to move toward.

One option is to create *long-term life goals*. A life goal might be to give one million dollars to God's kingdom, or to never weigh more than 180 pounds, or to launch a business you enjoy running and that provides you a healthy income until retirement.

Or you may choose to create *yearly goals*. A yearly goal could be giving 11 percent of all your income back to God, or to run a half-marathon, or to go back to school to get your MBA.

Personally, I tend to prefer *quarterly goals*. The smaller time frame eliminates the option of procrastinating. It forces me to jump into action and start accomplishing the goal immediately. And as I accomplish my quarterly goal, I find myself a step closer to moving toward my ultimate destination. So I look at where I want to go, and then decide on a critical step I can take in the next three months to move me closer to where I need to be. A goal for a quarter might be to redo your family budget, to lose ten pounds, to read a book on entrepreneurship, to read three books on parenting, to take your spouse out on twelve dates in the next twelve weeks, to do a spiritual retreat, to take a seminar on public speaking, to confess a struggle you've been having to two close friends, or to read through the four Gospels and rejoice again in who Jesus is.

If you do quarterly goals, you probably don't want to be juggling too many at one time. Less is more. If you have five to seven life journeys, I'd suggest having no more than one goal for each that you're intentionally working on at one time.

So what specific, measurable goals do you need to create?

Question Four: Why do you want to arrive at that destination and arrive at those goals?

In his book *Start with Why*,[4] Simon Sinek writes that what influences people to action, and to persist, is not understanding the *what* or the *how* but understanding the *why*. Leaders like Martin Luther King Jr. and Steve Jobs were inspiring because they started with why. It's true for you as well. What will move this from being a plan on paper to being your actual life is not the what or the how but the why.

So *why* do you want what you've put down on paper? What's the reason? How will you benefit if it really happens? How will others benefit?

I'd suggest that your why needs to include some sense of following God's plan for your life. God does have a plan for your life (see Jer. 29:11), and you don't want to make your own plan that leads you to miss out on his. And, by the way, God's plan for your life centers on him, not you (see Rom. 12:1–3; Col. 3:1–3, 17). So if your plan isn't focused on God and your greatest goal isn't to live for and please him, your plans and goals are too shortsighted, too self-centered, and too small.

So, take some time and answer the question: *Why?* It's the why that will get you started toward your destination and keep you motivated when the journey is difficult.

Day Four

Question Five: Where are you in each journey at this time?

In this step you'll take a long, honest look at yourself and put down on paper where you currently are in each journey. The answer may be encouraging or it may be disheartening. Either way, you need to know where you are now if you're going to get where you need to go.

Here's what I wrote at one of my quarterly reviews about my current location in my journey as a father to my kids:

> I'm not a good enough example of loving God and loving people. They know I love God and people, but I don't think they see enough passion in me.
>
> I do think Dawson and Marissa know I love them unconditionally, and that I love them too much to leave them the way they are.
>
> I believe in my kids, but at times I may be too focused on their faults and "improving" them as people.
>
> I'm available and around, but I am often too stressed in life and too easily stressed at home. At times I'm not that fun to be around.

Take some time to write down where you are in each journey right now.

Day Five

Question Six: What's the path to get you from where you are to where you want to be?

If I walk out of my house in Las Vegas, jump in my car, and just start driving, hoping that I end up in Miami, it's not likely to happen. In fact, there's almost no chance. To get there I need a plan, a map, or a GPS that shows me what roads to take.

We won't get where we want to be in life just because we want to get there. Hoping isn't enough. We need a plan. We need to know the roads that will move us toward our destination. Your initial attempt at making your plan will help you see how you'll get there, and every time you read it you'll find yourself recommitting to following that path.

Here's the path I wrote for my journey as a father to my kids:

I will lead and encourage my kids to have their own faith and relationship with God through Jesus, and to read the Bible and pray every day.

Every day I will pray for my kids and tell them that Jesus loves them and that I love them.

I will look for teachable moments to lovingly help my kids better know Jesus and what it means to follow him. I will graciously bring them back when they get off course.

I will make sure we have a "family fun night" every week.

I will take my family on a vacation every year, and at least one "weekend" getaway. I will institute lots of meaningful family traditions that will help bond us together.

I will do two years of one-on-one "discipling" with each child while they're in high school. We'll read books together, discuss the tough questions, and talk about life.

One way to think about these paths is that they're often habits you build into your life. Aristotle said, "We are what we repeatedly do. Excellence, then, is not an act but a habit." There's a lot of truth in that. In a sense, we are a bundle of habits. So what collection of habits would turn you into the kind of person you want to become?

As you discern them, come up with *triggers* that will help you engage in those habits. A ton of research has revealed that we're far more likely to practice new habits if we create triggers for them. For instance, recently I wanted to start running four days a week. To help myself, I put out my running clothes and sneakers the night before. Seeing all that when I wake up helps trigger the habit.

So what habits do you need, and what could help you trigger those habits?

Also think about *rewards* you can place in your life to celebrate actually doing those habits. Again, research tells us that when we strategically plan on celebrating when we practice our habits, there's an increased likelihood we'll actually practice them. The celebration doesn't have to be significant. I have a phone app that records how far I run each day. Getting to see how far I went and watching my total miles add up week by week makes me feel good and is enough celebration to help me put on those sneakers each morning.

So what habits do you need, what could help you to trigger those habits, and what rewards can you place in your life to celebrate actually doing those habits?

Day Six

Question Seven: *What are the speed bumps and roadblocks that will slow the journey to your destination?*

This isn't a fun question, but it's a realistic one. The journey won't be easy. If it were, everyone would live the lives they want to live. But the reality is that very few people do. *You* are going to do it, but it won't be easy. So why don't you at least acknowledge what you foresee as your speed bumps and roadblocks? That way when they come up you won't be surprised, and they'll be less likely to deter you.

It's not enough to just identify the obstacles. You need a plan for how to overcome them. You'll be much more levelheaded and capable of forming a better strategy now than when you are in the middle of difficulty.

Question Eight: *For each journey, who do you need to take with you?*

Often when you go on a road trip you have someone with you. And on each of the journeys that make up our lives, it may be helpful to have a companion. It might be a partner, a mentor, or someone you're mentoring. In this step decide and write down whom you need to take with you to help you get to each destination. For your journey with God, it might be a few accountability partners. For your journey with your spouse, it will obviously be your spouse, but it may also be a couple to mentor you both on how to do marriage right. For your health, it might be a physical trainer. For the impact you want to have through serving, it could be your pastor.

Day Seven

The Renegade Question

Once you've made your way through those questions, you'll probably need to do it again.

Why?

What I've proposed—these questions you'll be answering—are much like many other life-planning methods. As with those, if you follow this plan and truly apply it, it *will* help you to live a better life, a good life.

But will it lead you to a renegade life?

Because—remember—we're not trying to be respectable; we're trying to be risk-takers for Jesus. We're not trying to be dignified; we're going for dangerous. Not happy but holy. Not selfish but selfless. Not accomplished but adventurous.

And so, as you go through these questions, as you think about who you want to be, who you want your family to be, what your goals are, and what you want to accomplish with your life, you need to be asking yourself questions such as:

What would I do for God if resources were not an issue and I knew I could not fail?

How would I live if I really believed my life had supernatural power behind it?

What is the boldest thing I can imagine doing in this area of my life?

What about my life is inexplicable without knowing that I
  live for Jesus and have the Holy Spirit empowering me?

What in this plan cannot happen unless God is in it?

Thinking like that will lead you to a *renegade life plan*, and
hopefully into living the life of a renegade. It should change
some of the destinations and goals you set for yourself. Perhaps
instead of a goal of giving 10 percent back to God, you'll have
a goal of giving him 50 percent. Maybe you'll have a goal of
your family living together in a third world country for at least
one month. You might dream about spending one hour of each
day in an intimate time with God, or running a marathon, or
leading one hundred people to Christ, or starting a business
that will employ one hundred people, or launching a ministry
in your church to help an impoverished minority people group
in your town.

You only get one life here on earth, and God has invited you
to live it with him and for him. He's called you to something
radical, and through your intimacy with him, he can equip and
empower you to have great influence for him. So don't focus on
what you've already done, what others have done, or what you
think you can do. With him, anything is possible, and he can
do more in and through you than you dare imagine. So dream
big, and make your life plan a renegade life plan.

Living Your Plan

If you do this, you'll have a plan. Now you have to start living it.

I would encourage you to read it every day for at least the first
month after you write it. You want to burn it into your brain.
It's probably not the way you've been living, so there's a kind of
conversion or rebirth that needs to happen. So read your plan
each morning when you wake up or every night before bed until
you're sick of reading it.

After that first month your plan can't just sit and collect
dust. Get it out every quarter and do a review. I use this time to

update my answers for the "Where are you in each journey right now?" question. Because I use quarterly goals, I also evaluate how well I did in reaching them. Then I create new goals for the next three months of my life.

How you implement your plan is up to you, but implementing is not an option. Living the same way you've lived isn't an option. A halfhearted, boring, but decent and respectable life is no longer an option. God is calling you to something better. He's calling you to a full life. He's calling you to a dangerous faith. He's calling you to become a renegade.

Read This Book with Your Church

There you are, sitting and reading this book. You're crying. You're laughing. Milk is coming out of your nose. (Go get a towel!) You're inspired. You're challenged. There's only one thing missing: someone else. Anyone else. You have thoughts you want to share, questions you want to ask, applications you want to make. But you have no one to talk to.

Reading a book is typically a solitary act, but it doesn't have to be. It *shouldn't* be. One of the best ways to engage the content of this book is in a group setting. So go against the norm, be a renegade, and read this in a group.

How? Well . . .

It can be as simple as you and a friend, or a couple of friends, getting together in a living room, a coffee shop, or a Laundromat and processing a chapter or two a week.

Or . . . if you're in a small group at your church, you could suggest *Renegade* as your next study. The questions in the next appendix should provide for a lively and life-transforming discussion.

Or . . . if you're a pastor, you can get your whole church moving toward becoming renegades (and how cool would that be for your people and your church?!). You could have your entire church read the book, or you could even do a *Renegade* series. Go to www.renegadebook.org to find everything needed for a *Renegade* series—sermons, videos, graphics, and more. You can also get case quantities of *Renegade* at deep discounts. And Baker Publishing is giving 10 percent of *Renegade* case quantity sales to support Vince's church, Verve Church. So when you buy a case, not only will you be helping your church, you'll be helping Verve Church in the heart of Sin City.

At www.renegadebook.org you'll also find all kinds of fun and interesting "extras." For instance, don't miss the "From the Cutting Room Floor" section—deleted sentences and paragraphs from Vince's first draft of this book.

So what have we learned?

Reading *Renegade* alone? Good!

Reading it with some friends or your small group? Great!

Reading it with your entire church? God has not yet invented a word to describe how perfect and amazing that is. But if he does, we'll let you know.

Discussion Questions

Use the following questions to discuss and apply each chapter with a friend or a small group.

Chapter 1: Beware the Fire-Breathing Atheist

1. Vince first encountered Jesus when he began reading the Bible at age twenty. How did you first encounter Jesus? How old were you? Where did it happen? Who taught you?

2. Think back on the first picture of Jesus you developed in your mind.

   What about it was pretty inaccurate?

   What about it was more accurate?

3. Vince calls Jesus a homeless king of a wrong-side-up kingdom who was viewed as a crazy man leading an uncivilized revolution.

   Does anything about that description bother you?

   What about the description appeals to you?

4. Vince writes: "People who said yes in the Bible had their lives inverted. They realized that everything they had been

taught, everything they had lived, was wrong. They went
from selfish to selfless, from grudge-inspired thoughts of
revenge to loving their enemies through acts of kindness,
from playing it safe to playing it dangerous."

In what ways do you think your life still needs to be
inverted?

Think about it this way: If God told you there was
something about your view of him, or of his kingdom,
or of what it means to follow him that needed to change
drastically, what do you think it would be?

5. If a renegade is someone who rejects normal (because
normal isn't really working for *anyone*) to find what's
right so they can truly live for God, could you call yourself
a renegade?

6. What do you think is the primary thing holding you back
from fully giving yourself to God and living the life of a
renegade?

7. How could you (with God) overcome the one thing that's
holding you back the most?

Chapter 2: Don't Live a Cheap Imitation

1. Have you ever bought an imitation of something (maybe
the generic version of a product) and been disappointed?
What was it?

2. Vince asks some questions in chapter 2 that are worth
thinking through.

How did you spend yesterday? What were the main
events of the day? When you returned home, what did
you spend your time doing?

Looking back at that day, what about it would you say
was truly God-centered? Joy-filled? Purpose-driven?
Would you describe anything you did as adventurous,
risky, or dangerous?

Is there anything happening in your life that truly
requires faith? Are you doing anything that is only

explainable by the fact that you believe in God and follow Jesus?

Is this all there is?

3. Do your answers to those questions make you fear you may be living a cheap imitation of following Jesus rather than the real thing?

4. Can you think of anyone in the Bible who truly lived a life of faith and was bored with his or her life?

5. Of all the people you know, who is someone you'd say is truly living a life of faith? What do you admire about that person? What about that person's life could you apply to your own life?

6. The word *renegade* is often used to describe people who reject their religion. Vince asks, "What if to truly find God and an adventurous life we need to abandon our religion? I'm not suggesting we walk away from God or the church or other believers. I'm saying that we leave behind the religious approach to God most of us take, which leads us to a cheap imitation of following him. We may not have to abandon our faith but rather abandon our way of doing faith—the way of faith we learned from our family, our friends, and what we've known before. We may have to go a bit rogue to find a religion-free relationship with God that leads to true intimacy with him and true influence in this world."

Do you agree or disagree, and why?

What about your current way of doing faith might you need to abandon to find true intimacy with God and to have true influence in the world?

Chapter 3: Overcome the Bad Start

1. Chapter 3 presents the possibility that our relationship with God may have not gotten off to a good start because of a misunderstanding of what the Christian life is all about. Which of these common misunderstandings may

have been true of you when you first started? And why do you think you fell into that misunderstanding?

"The Christian life is all about getting saved from hell."
"The Christian life is about religion—it gives me God's rules and boundaries for how to live life right."
"God is someone to know about. I am supposed to learn the Bible."
"God is available to me and will give me things if I am faithful to him and I pray for them."

2. Vince states, "The Christian life is about intimacy with God that leads to influence in the world." Would you agree or disagree with that statement? Why?

3. Vince presents a very radical version of intimacy with God: making God your entire life and intensely seeking to have God pour himself into you. He backs this up by showing in the Bible how God commands us to love him, serve him, obey him, and worship him with *all* of ourselves. Could you honestly say that this is where you're at as far as your intimacy with God goes? Why or why not?

4. What practical steps could you take to increase your passion for and intimacy with God?

5. Will you take those steps this week? If not, why not? What would stop you?

6. Vince also presents a very radical version of influence on the world: we can't be selfish with what we have from God and we need to intensely seek to pour ourselves out for others. He backs this up by showing in the Bible how we're commanded to love and serve others. Could you honestly say that this is where you're at as far as your influence on the world goes? Why or why not?

7. What practical steps could you take to increase your passion for and influence on the world?

8. Will you take those steps this week? If not, why not? What would stop you?

9. Vince writes, "Intimacy without influence is insular. Influence without intimacy is impotent. We need God pouring

into us so we can be poured out for others. Without intimacy with God, we have little (if anything) to give." How have you seen this to be true in the church today? How have you seen it in your life?

10. What might your life look like if you had intimacy with God that led you to influence in the world?

Chapter 4: Search in the Right Parking Garage

1. Have you ever lost your car in a parking garage or parking lot? If not, what else have you lost? Do you have a fun story to share? Share it!

2. Vince states that most Christians think the Christian life is about growth. We seek spiritual growth, we become upset if we're not growing, and we change churches to find one that will help us grow. Where have you seen this assumption?

3. Vince goes on to say that it's not about growth; it's about love. What do you think would be some of the differences between a person who thinks life is about growing spiritually and someone who thinks life is about loving God and loving people?

4. Consider this statement: "When we make it about growth we live self-indulgent and boring lives. When we make it about love we live selfless and adventurous lives." Do you agree or disagree? Why?

5. What impresses you about the example of Mother Antonia?

6. Something must be different about her view of God and of the Christian life to make her live in such a radical way. What do you think it is?

7. In what way do you think she's an example of being poured into by God and poured out for others?

8. You're probably not going to go live in a Mexican prison, but what from Mother Antonia's example can you apply to your life?

Chapter 5: You Can't Have Faith without Risk

1. What is the biggest risk you've ever taken for God?
2. What gave you the courage to take such a risk?
3. Vince makes the case that there is no faith without risk, and even goes so far as to say that faith *is* risk.
     Have you ever thought of faith that way?
     Do you agree or disagree? Why?
4. Hebrews 11 presents God's "hall of fame" of faith, with each faith-filled hero presented as someone who took a risk for God. Which of the people mentioned in Hebrews 11 really stands out to you? Why?
5. If it's true that "You cannot play it safe and please God," how pleasing would you say your life is to God? Or, in other words, how safe are you playing it?
6. What do you think was the biggest difference between David and all the other Israelites who refused to fight Goliath?
7. What do you think is the biggest difference between Dallas and all the Christians who would never consider quitting their job and severely reducing their lifestyle in order to help homeless people?
8. What do you think it would take for you to start "playing it dangerous"?
9. If you knew you could not fail, what is one thing you'd love to do for God?
10. What if the only way to fail is through not attempting it at all? Then your fear of failure would actually be causing you to fail. So . . . why not (in the immortal words of Nike) just do it?

Chapter 6: Stare Down the Risk

1. What about the Katie Davis story really struck you? Why?
2. Vince claims that the secret to overcoming fear is to base your willingness to risk on the potential return. Where

have you seen this play out in your life? Have you ever taken a risk because the potential reward was so great?

3. Do you think it's true that most Christians play it safe because they stare at the risk instead of the potential return?

4. How might that be true for Christians who:

Refuse to tithe?

Refuse to volunteer?

Refuse to share their faith?

Refuse to go on a mission trip?

Refuse to invite their friends to church?

5. In chapter 5 we saw that God tells us in the book of Hebrews that we cannot please him without faith. We looked at Hebrews 11:1, "Now faith is confidence in what we hope for and assurance about what we do not see," and saw several examples from Hebrews 11 where the key to living by faith and taking a risk was what the person was looking at. In other words, these heroes of the faith looked past the fear and saw the reward.

What about you? What have you been looking at?

If you knew you could not fail, what is one thing you'd love to do for God?

What are the fears you may have been looking at that are involved in doing that one thing?

Do you feel as if staring at those fears has held you back?

What is the reward of that one thing? What is the potential return?

How could you stare at the potential return?

How might it move you to act?

Chapter 7: Trust the Catcher

1. Watching trapeze artists, Henri Nouwen observed that the flyer wouldn't dare take the risk without the assurance that he would be caught; the catcher is really the one who allows the fantastic to happen. He wrote, "If we are to

take risks, to be free, in the air, in life, we have to know there's a catcher."

Do you normally think about God as someone who would catch you if you were to fall?

If not, why not? What do you think might have shaped your image of God as being someone who either isn't able to catch you or doesn't care enough to catch you? If you do think of God as your catcher, how does that make you feel? What assurance does that give you?

2. Would you agree that our two greatest needs are for security (the need to feel safe) and significance (the need to feel your life matters)? Why or why not?

3. Where do you see the need for security at play in your life?

4. Where do you see the need for significance at play in your life?

5. Vince contends that our two basic needs are often in conflict because to live lives of significance we typically need to do something that threatens our security. Looking back at your life, how has your need for security perhaps held you back from taking an action that would have given your life more significance?

6. The answer, according to Vince, is to make God our source of security. Because our security in him can never be threatened, this will free us to take the risks needed to live lives of significance. What would it look like, practically, to make God your source of security?

7. Read Psalm 31:1–5.

How does David, the author of this psalm, view God? What does it look like for him to make God his source of security?

8. This week, what might it look like for you to trust the catcher?

Chapter 8: Get God in Your Gut

1. What is your favorite word? Why?

2. If you were put in Elizabeth Morris's situation—the mother of a son killed by a drunk driver—do you think you could do what she did (forgive the drunk driver, then lead him to Christ and basically adopt him)?

   If you're not sure you could, think about this: What does Elizabeth Morris have that you don't? She's not superhuman, so what do you think it is about her that allowed her to show such grace?

3. Jesus is repeatedly shown as having gut-wrenching compassion for people who were in need, were hurting, and (especially) were disconnected from their heavenly Father.

   On a scale of 1 to 10, where would you say your compassion level is right now? (How much compassion do you have for others—especially the needy, hurting, and disconnected from God?)

   What could you do to raise your compassion level?

4. The story of CiCi shows someone having compassion for a specific group of people because of her own past experiences. What from your past (your experiences, your hurts, your sin) raises up compassion in you for a specific issue or group of people?

5. If your life hasn't been all you want it to be (if it hasn't been very renegade), do you think that may be the result of a lack of passionate compassion for other people? Why or why not?

6. Maybe the best strategy to raise our level of compassion is to do acts of compassion. (Perhaps our feelings follow our actions, not just the other way around.) Just in case that may be true, what act of compassion will you take this week?

Chapter 9: Discover Your Calling

1. What are your three favorite movies?

2. What common thread do those movies have? And how might that common thread be a hint at your calling?

3. Have you ever asked God to reveal his calling on your life and really listened for his answer?

   If so, in what way did he lead you?

   If you didn't feel as if God told you anything, why do you think that is?

4. How might your past (perhaps your experiences or your pain) be a key to figuring out what you should do with your life?

5. What makes you angry with a righteous indignation? Is there some wrong that exists in this world that you can't tolerate and would love to do something about?

6. What makes you happy? Is there something that, when you do it, you feel as if it was what you were *made* to do?

7. If you were to form a Clearness Committee to help you discern God's calling on your life, who might you ask?

8. Have you ever taken a "test" to help you determine your strengths and gifts? What strengths and gifts do other people see in you and have mentioned to you?

9. What "low-cost probe" could you do to help you try out a new calling without fully committing to it?

Chapter 10: Caution Your Calling

1. Have you ever ignored a caution and paid for it? Do you have a funny or interesting story to share?

2. Have you ever had the experience of knowing you're following God and living out his calling on your life, but it's difficult or draining or depressing? What happened? How did it feel?

3. Have you had the experience of serving God in your calling but having to wait to see the results? How difficult was it to wait?

4. Why do you think God often gives us an incomplete picture of our calling and our future? Why might that be for the best?

5. Vince makes the case that once you find your calling and start living it, you will often fail in it. That may be a

surprise, since there's an assumption that our calling will
come naturally to us. Why do you think we may struggle
when we first start living out our calling? Have you ever
experienced this?

6. When we think of people who have a "calling" from God,
we think of people who do dramatic things in the world.
But we all have a calling from God. They're just not all
so dramatic. How do you think having a less-dramatic
calling might prevent someone from pursuing it?

7. Vince claims that when we discover and live out our calling we become a target of Satan.

Does that make sense to you? Why or why not?

Have you ever started engaging in your calling and
then had the experience that there were forces working
against you? What happened?

Chapter 11: Avoid Your Other Calling

1. Vince writes that our life mission is to love God, love
people, and turn the world upside down, but points out
that a lot of people adopt another calling. Their lives become too focused on something that doesn't have eternal
significance.

What is a "shadow mission" that you find yourself
giving your life to, but is not really your calling?

2. What do you think might cause someone to live out a
calling that isn't God's true calling on their life?

3. How have you seen this play out in your life?

4. If someone doesn't embrace their calling, how might their
life be negatively impacted?

5. How might the world be negatively impacted?

6. Vince admits that it's easier for him to hide in his office
than be out with hurting people. Where do you find yourself hiding from your calling?

7. What might embracing the fear look like for you in regard
to living out your true calling?

Chapter 12: Set Yourself on Fire in the Darkness

1. Jesus called himself the light of the world. What are some examples in the Bible where we see Jesus going into the darkness so he could serve his purpose as light?

2. Read Matthew 5:14–16. Christians are to be the light of the world, and light can only serve its purpose if it's shining in the darkness.

3. Why do you think it's so easy for Christians to stay in the light, hanging out with other Christians and avoiding both dangerous places and people who are far from God?

4. Do you think Vince may have gone too far in his attempt to be light in the darkness by being a part of a comedy show?

5. Religious people thought Jesus went too far in his attempt to be light in the darkness because he was always hanging out with sinners.

6. Do you think perhaps a Christian has to go to what seems like the brink of "too far" before they've gone far enough?

7. Jesus was called a friend of sinners (see Matt. 11:19). Are you close enough to people who are far from God that you could be called a friend of sinners?

8. Do people see the light of God shining through you? Do they notice something different about you?

    If so, how do they respond?

    If not, what do you think might be the key to changing that?

Chapter 13: Lead with Love

1. Tommy used his motorcycle riding to develop friendships with other motorcyclists and his love of tattoos to make friends with tattoo artists. Which of your hobbies or interests could you use to build relationships with people who are far from God?

2. Do you agree that everyone is looking to be loved and looking for truth to live by? Why or why not?

3. Do you agree that two of the most significant things Christians have to offer are love and truth? Why or why not?

4. In our culture, Christians are known for proclaiming and fighting for truth, but not so much for their love. Why do you think so many Christians have focused on truth more than love?

5. Most non-Christians know what Christians believe but don't know them as people. They know the truth Christians stand for, but haven't seen the love they're supposed to be marked by.

   The Bible teaches us that we need to make truth attractive (see Titus 2:10). If a non-Christian told you that they refused to turn to Jesus because Jesus's followers haven't made his truth attractive, how would you respond?

6. How do you think "leading with love" could be the antidote for the problem so many Christians have created? In what ways have you seen that happen?

7. Who are some of the people without Jesus whom God has put in your life?

8. How could you lead with love with each of them this week? What are some practical things you could do to show them God's love, build your relationship, and open them up to God's truth?

9. Once you have led with love and are given the opportunity to share truth, what do you think is an effective way to share Jesus with someone who doesn't really know him? How could you make it very clear? And how could you make it compelling?

Chapter 14: Renegade Profiles

1. What sticks out for you in Travis's story? What do you think makes him a renegade? What can you apply from his life to yours?

2. What hit you from Monica's story? Her first trip to Vietnam was inspired by a desire to use her nursing skills to

serve other people for God. What skills (job, hobby, or other) do you have that you might be able to use to influence the world for God?

3. What about George impresses you? What principles can you learn from his life and apply to your life?
4. What did you learn from Matt's story about the life of a renegade? What past hurts do you have to deal with? How might those hurts help you minister to others?
5. What about Heidi's life caught your attention? Heidi saw something God was doing in Las Vegas and realized it was something God could use her to do in Savannah. Is there anything you've seen God doing that maybe he could use you to do?
6. What hit you about Ethan, Matt, Doug, and Ryan's story? In their blog post they speak of never being so uncomfortable and never feeling so close to God. Is it possible that your comfort is keeping you from feeling close to God? How could you get uncomfortable in your life and use that to get closer to God?

Chapter 15: Hear What You Don't Want to Hear

1. Vince says that one of the most common questions pastors receive is, "How can I hear God's voice?" Is this a question you've wondered about? Why or why not?
2. When have you struggled to hear God?
3. Do you think it's possible that one of the reasons you haven't heard from God is because you really don't want to hear what he has to say? Why or why not?
4. What do you think are some of the reasons God never tells anyone in the Bible what they want to hear, and never gives an easy assignment?
5. If you were Ajai Lall and God told you to speak with rifles pointed at you, what would be your initial thoughts? How do you think you'd respond to God?

6. Is there anything you feel God has told you to do that you haven't? What is it? Why did you say no?
7. How often do you ask God to speak to you and then make yourself quiet and really listen? If you were to do that, is there anything you think God might say to you?
8. To be a renegade you need to be willing to hear what you don't want to hear and to obey God no matter what. Are you willing?

Chapter 16: Spend Your Time Waiting

1. What is your favorite thing to cook? To eat? How is "waiting" one of the ingredients of that dish?
2. Did it surprise you to find out that God tells us to wait at least forty-three times in the Old Testament alone? Why do you think this is so common?
3. Psalm 27:14 tells us to "wait for the LORD; be strong and take heart and wait for the LORD." Why do you think being strong and taking heart are necessary when we're waiting?
4. In this chapter we saw a long list of people from the Bible who were promised something by God but then had to wait. Did any of the stories really stick out to you? What did you learn?
5. When is a time you've had to wait for something you've really wanted?
6. What are you currently wanting but have to wait for?
7. Vince suggests that while we wait we should wrestle with God (be authentic with him and honestly struggle) *and* embrace God (draw close to him and draw comfort from him). Which of those is more difficult for you? Why?

Chapter 17: Break the Silence

1. The Israelites in Elijah's time had drifted from their devotion to God. What are some of the factors you think lead people to drift from their devotion to God?

2. When have you experienced a loss of devotion or passion for God? What do you think caused it?

3. The Israelites continued to think of themselves as God's people but at the same time were worshiping Baal. We tend to "two-time" God in the same way. We give our hearts, devotion, money, energy, and time to *things* as if they were of ultimate importance. For you it might be success, sex, popularity, money, a girlfriend or boyfriend, food, partying, your image, or your job. Be honest: What other gods do you worship?

4. In what ways have you "bled" for these other gods?

5. How long would you say you've worshiped these other gods? What do you think led you to seek your fulfillment, satisfaction, and joy in those things?

6. What are the problems with having more than one God? Why is it bad for you? Bad for God? Bad for the world?

7. We tend to seek "other things" and hope God is okay with it so we can have him too. But in Matthew 6:33 Jesus tells us, "But seek first his kingdom and his righteousness, and all these things will be given to you as well." Why do you think that is the right order?

8. What changes would have to take place in your life for you to truly worship God above everything else?

9. Do you think it's possible that giving your heart to something other than God is what has kept you from living the life of a renegade for God?

Chapter 18: Eat the Whole Burger

1. Where in your life have you shown perseverance and accomplished something great?

2. When is a time you've quit on something? What did you quit on? What was the result?

3. If you could go back to the thing you quit, what would you do differently?

4. Vince provides examples of people who achieved greatness only through endurance: Michael Jordan, U2, and Steve Jobs. Which of those stories spoke to you the most? Why?

5. John Wesley accomplished great things for God, but only after experiencing persecution. Have you ever been persecuted for trying to do something for God? How so?

6. William Carey accomplished great things for God, but only after experiencing great personal loss. Have you ever had to fight through personal loss to continue down God's path for you? How so?

7. Adoniram Judson accomplished great things for God, but only after years of seeing *no* results. Have you ever had to persevere through a long time of no results? How so?

8. Vince says we quit because anything great is hard and we give ourselves the option of quitting. Where have you seen this in your life?

9. What are some of the things that are too important for you to give yourself the option of quitting?

10. In what ways might you be tempted to quit living a renegade life of having intimacy with God?

Chapter 19: Go Out in a Blaze of Glory

1. What do you think of the idea of imagining your funeral to help you better live your life? Does it seem morbid to you? Wise?

2. Someday you're going to be in a box. You can do everything you can to ignore that as a morbid reality, or you can allow it to change everything for you. Which will it be?

3. How did the story of Warren Schmidt speak to you?

4. Can you picture going through the motions for a lifetime like Warren Schmidt and then dying with regrets for what you didn't do? How does the thought make you feel?

5. Vince writes, "Renegades don't have much remorse when they look back at their lives. Sure, they go through some tumultuous times, experience some discouragement,

maybe wish they had trusted God a little more. But they've lived the life of a renegade, walking alone in faith when necessary, being poured into by God and poured out for him, and taking risks for him."

Can you picture that being your life story? Why or why not?

How would it make you feel to have that be your life?

6. What needs to change today for you to be able to look back at your life with no regrets?

7. You have finished the book. But regardless of what you've read, if you don't apply it you will be like the duck who waddled home. So:

What will you do to grow your intimacy with God?

What will you do to increase your influence in the world?

What risks will you take because you believe God is calling you to take them?

It may be a lonely road, a journey not many are willing to take, but because you have God walking with you, you can do it. You can be a renegade. And remember, your faith was not meant to be safe.

Notes

Chapter 3 Overcome the Bad Start

1. See Mark 12:30; Luke 10:27.
2. See Deuteronomy 4:29; Jeremiah 29:13.
3. See Deuteronomy 10:12; 11:13; Joshua 22:5.
4. See Deuteronomy 26:16; 30:2.
5. See Psalms 9:1; 86:12.
6. See Deuteronomy 13:3.
7. See, for instance, James 1:22–27; 2:14–26.
8. Matthew 25:35–36.
9. Matthew 28:19–20.
10. See, for instance, John 15:1–17.

Chapter 4 Search in the Right Parking Garage

1. See, for instance, Luke 10:25–28.
2. Johnny Dodd, "From Beverly Hills to Mexican Jail," *People* 63, no. 20 (May 23, 2005): http://www.people.com/people/archive/article/0,, 20147637,00.html.
3. Ibid.
4. Ibid.

Chapter 5 You Can't Have Faith without Risk

1. Hebrews 11:32–39.
2. See Matthew 25:14–30.
3. I think I first heard this idea stated in this way by Erwin McManus.
4. See Romans 6:3–11; 8:31–39; Galatians 2:20.
5. I first told some of Dallas's story in my book *I Became a Christian and All I Got Was This Lousy T-Shirt* (Grand Rapids: Baker, 2008).

Chapter 6 Stare Down the Risk

1. You can learn more about Katie Davis and her ministry at www.amazima.org and in her book, *Kisses from Katie: A Story of Relentless Love and Redemption* (Nashville: Howard Books, 2011).
2. I believe I first heard this illustration of this principle from Craig Groeschel.
3. 1 Samuel 17:26.
4. Hebrews 11:10, emphasis mine.
5. Hebrews 11:27, emphasis mine.
6. Hebrews 11:13, emphasis mine.

Chapter 7 Trust the Catcher

1. Henri J. M. Nouwen, *Sabbatical Journey: The Diary of His Final Year* (New York: Crossroad Publishing, 1998), 2ff.
2. Henri Nouwen as quoted in *Angels Over the Net*, directed by The Company (New York: Spark Productions, 1995), DVD.
3. See, for instance, Larry Crabb, *Effective Biblical Counseling: A Model for Helping Caring Christians Become Capable Counselors* (Grand Rapids: Zondervan, 1977).
4. See Psalms 2:12; 5:11; 7:1; 9:9; 11:1; 18:30; 25:20; 31:1; 34:22; Nahum 1:7; Matthew 11:28.
5. See Romans 8:28–39.
6. See 1 John 4:18.

Chapter 8 Get God in Your Gut

1. See http://www.people.com/people/archive/article/0,,20091574,00.html and http://articles.latimes.com/1985-09-01/news/mn-25735_1_drunk-driver.
2. Matthew 9:36.
3. We see Jesus have this *splagna* reaction many times. For some other examples, see Matthew 14:14; 15:32; and 20:34.
4. Matthew 9:36.
5. Matthew 9:37–38.

Chapter 9 Discover Your Calling

1. Frederick Buechner, *Beyond Words: Daily Readings in the ABC's of Faith* (San Francisco: HarperOne: 2004), 405–6.
2. See Romans 12:1–7; 1 Corinthians 12.
3. See, for instance, www.strengthsfinder.com.

Chapter 10 Caution Your Calling

1. Romans 12:2.
2. See 1 Peter 5:8.
3. 2 Chronicles 16:9.
4. See John 10:10.

5. See 1 John 4:4.
6. Again, see John 10:10.

Chapter 11 Avoid Your Other Calling

1. John Ortberg, *When the Game Is Over, It All Goes Back in the Box* (Grand Rapids: Zondervan, 2007), 170–71.

Chapter 12 Set Yourself on Fire in the Darkness

1. John 8:12.
2. John 9:5.
3. John 12:45–46.
4. John 20:21.
5. Matthew 5:14–16.
6. See John 1:4–5.
7. *Man on Fire*, directed by Tony Scott (Twentieth Century Fox, 2004), DVD.

Chapter 13 Lead with Love

1. Tommy is also starting a ministry called Tattoo Church. Check it out at www.tattoochurch.org.
2. See, for instance, John 1:14.
3. Luke 19:5.
4. Luke 19:8.
5. The best treatment of this topic I've read is in John Burke's *No Perfect People Allowed* (Grand Rapids: Zondervan, 2007).

Chapter 14 Renegade Profiles

1. *The AC Project*, http://theac.org/blog.

Chapter 15 Hear What You Don't Want to Hear

1. Preaching & Teaching Convention, Ozark Christian College, Joplin, Missouri, February 21–23, 2011.
2. Henry Blackaby and Claude King, *Experiencing God: How to Live the Full Adventure of Knowing and Doing the Will of God* (Nashville: Broadman & Holman, 1994).
3. See 1 John 2:5.
4. As told by Mark Batterson in *Primal: A Quest for the Lost Soul of Christianity* (Colorado Springs: Multnomah, 2009), 140–41.

Chapter 16 Spend Your Time Waiting

1. Psalm 27:14.
2. Psalm 37:7.
3. Isaiah 64:4.

4. Lewis B. Smedes, *Standing on the Promises: Keeping Hope Alive for a Tomorrow We Cannot Control* (Nashville: Thomas Nelson, 1998), 41–42.

5. Habakkuk 3:17–19.

Chapter 17 Break the Silence

1. See 1 Kings 16:29–33.

2. Again, see 1 Kings 16:29–33.

3. 1 Kings 18:21.

4. 1 Kings 18:36–37.

5. 1 Kings 18:38.

6. 1 Kings 18:39.

Chapter 19 Go Out in a Blaze of Glory

1. *About Schmidt*, directed by Alexander Payne (2002; New Line Cinema, 2003), DVD.

2. *Malatya: The Story of the First Martyrs of the Modern Turkish Church*, www.malatyafilm.com.

3. Gavan Daws, *Holy Man: Father Damien of Molokai* (Honolulu: University of Hawaii Press, 1984).

The Renegade Life Plan

1. Psalm 90:5–6.

2. Psalm 90:12.

3. Gary Kasparov, *How Life Imitates Chess: Making the Right Moves, from the Board to the Boardroom* (New York: Bloomsbury, 2008), 18.

4. Simon Sinek, *Start with Why: How Great Leaders Inspire Everyone to Take Action* (New York: Portfolio Hardcover, 2009).

Vince Antonucci became a Christian out of a completely non-Christian background, which has led him to start two churches for people who don't like church. He was the founding pastor of Forefront Church in Virginia Beach, Virginia, where 72 percent of the people attending were previously unchurched non-Christians. Vince then moved to Las Vegas where he started a new church, Verve, in the heart of Sin City, just off the Vegas Strip. He blogs at www.vinceantonucci.com. He speaks and coaches on having a unique church with vision clarity for Auxano.com. Vince is the author of *I Became a Christian and All I Got Was This Lousy T-Shirt* (2008), *Guerrilla Lovers* (2010), and *Renegade* (2013). He loves spending time with his best friends—his wife, Jennifer, and kids, Dawson and Marissa.

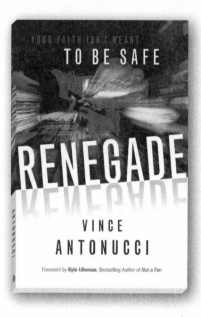